Oaths
of
Allegiance

in

Colonial
New England

By

Charles Evans

HERITAGE BOOKS
2026

HERITAGE BOOKS

AN IMPRINT OF HERITAGE BOOKS, INC.

Books, CDs, and more—Worldwide

For our listing of thousands of titles see our website
at
www.HeritageBooks.com

A Facsimile Reprint
Published 2026 by
HERITAGE BOOKS, INC.
Publishing Division
5810 Ruatan Street
Berwyn Heights, MD 20740

Originally published:
Worcester, Massachusetts
1922

Reprinted from the Proceedings of the
American Antiquarian Society
for October, 1921

International Standard Book Number
Paperbound: 978-0-7884-2754-1

OATHS OF ALLEGIANCE
IN COLONIAL NEW ENGLAND

THE antiquity of the custom of giving and taking Oaths, or the debatable questions of their observance being a religious or legal ceremony, and whether the moral or political aspect has the greater effect upon the minds of men, are subjects with which this paper has nothing to do.

And as the substance of Oaths for particular officers is to engage them to a faithful discharge of their places and trusts to the best of their ability, it has been considered, in general, unnecessary to give them, especially as these offices carry with them the assumption that the general Oaths required of all citizens have first been complied with. No Oaths of office were administered or required in the New Plymouth Colony, the power of the Church being, in effect, superior to the civil power.

For the main purpose of this paper it will not be necessary to go further back in history than to the reign of James the First, of England, 1603-1625, during which time the providences of God directed the course of the voyage of the Pilgrims away from the Colony of Virginia to their settlement at Plymouth in New England, in December, 1620; or to carry the subject beyond the time, in the short-lived reign of James the Second, 1685-1689, when, in December, 1686, Sir Edmund Andros, knight, arrived in Boston with a commission to govern New England, and the Colonial period of New England came to an end.

In England.

When Henry the Eighth renounced the authority of
the Pope, in 1534, an Act of Parliament was obtained
declaring him the only supreme head of the Church in
England on the earth; and utterly abolishing the
authority of the Roman Pontiff within the British
Dominions. To give effect to this Act there was
further enacted:

The Oath of Supremacy

I, A. B. do utterly testifie and declare in my Conscience, that
the Kings Highness is the only Supream Governour of this
Realm, and of all other His Highness Dominions and Countries,
as well in all Spiritual and Ecclesiastical things (or causes) as
Temporal: And that no Forraign Prince, Person, Prelate, State,
or Potentate, hath, or ought to have any jurisdiction, power,
superiority, preheminence or authority, Ecclesiastical or
Spiritual within this Realm: and therefore I do utterly renounce
and forsake all forreign jurisdiction, powers, superioritie, and
authorities, and do promise that from henceforth I shall bear
Faith and true Allegiance to the Kings Highness, His Heirs and
lawful Successors, and (to my power) shall assist and defend all
jurisdiction, priviledge, preheminence, & authority granted or
belonging to the Kings Highness, His Heirs and Successors, and
united and annexed to the imperial Crown of the Realm. So
help me God, &c.

The Act of Supremacy which broke the power of the
Roman Catholic Church in England, under Henry the
Eighth, and his successor, Edward the Sixth, was repealed under Mary Tudor, and revived under Eliza-
beth, in 1558. Following the Gunpowder Plot, James
the First, in 1605, had enacted an Oath of Allegiance,
also, which all British subjects were required to take.
This Oath of "submission and obedience to the King as
a temporal Sovereign, independent of any other power
upon earth" contained no acknowledgment of the
King as the head of the Church, and, by this omission,
Roman Catholics could take it without denying the
supremacy of the Pope in spiritual affairs:

TENOR OF THE OATH OF ALLEGIANCE, &C. TO BE TAKEN AND
SUBSCRIBED BY RECUSANTS

I. A.B. doe truely and sincerely acknowledge pfesse testifie and declare in my Conscience before God and the Worlde, That our Soveraigne Lorde Kinge James is lawfull and rightfull King of this Realme and of all other his Majesties Dominions and Countries; And that the Pope, neither of himselfe nor by any Authority of the Churche or Sea of Rome, or by any other meanes with any other, hath any Power or Authoritye to depose the King or to dispose any of his Majesties Kingdomes or Dominions, or to authorize any Forraigne Prince to invade or annoy hym or his Countries, or to discharge any of his Subjects of their Allegiaunce and Obedience to his Majestie, or to give Licence or Leave to any of them to beare Armes raise Tumult or to offer any violence or hurte to his Majestie Royall Pson State or Government or to any of his Majesties Subjects within his Majesties Dominions. Also I doe sweare from my heart, that notwithstanding any Declaraĉon or Sentence of Excommunicaĉon or Deprivaĉon made or graunted or to be made or graunted by the Pope or his Successors, or by any Authoritie derived or p̄tended to be derived from hym or his Sea against the saide King his Heires or Successors, or any Absolution of the saide Subjects from theire Obedience; I will beare Faithe and true Allegiaunce to his Majestie his Heires and Successors, and hym or them will defend to the uttermost of my power against all Conspiracies and Attempts whatsoever which shalbe made against his or theire persons theire Crowne and Dignitie by reason or colour of any. such Sentence or Declaraĉon or otherwise, and will doe my best endevour to disclose and make knowen unto his Majestie his Heires and Successors all Treasons and traiterous Conspiracies which I shall knowe or heare of to be against hym or any of them. And I doe further sweare, That I doe from my heart abhor, detest and abjure as impious and hereticall this damnable Doctrine and Position, that Princes which be excōmunicated or deprived by the Pope may be deposed or murthered by theire Subjects or any other whosoever. And I doe beleeve and in my Conscience am resolved, that neither the Pope nor any pson whatsoever hath power to absolve me of this Oath or any parte therof, which I acknowledge by good and full Authoritye to be lawfully ministered unto mee, and doe renounce all Pardons and Dispensaĉons to the contrarie; And all these things I do plainly and sincerely acknowledge and sweare, according to these expresse wordes by me spoken, and according to the playne and cōmon sense and understanding of the same wordes, without any equivocaĉon or mentall evasion or secret reservaçon whatsoever; And I doe make this recogniçon and acknowledgment heartily willingly and truly upon the true Faithe of a Christian: So help me God. Unto which Oath so taken, the saide pson shall subscribe his or her Name or Marke. [1605.]

Both of these Oaths were commanded during the reign of Charles the First, 1625-1649.

By the third Charter of the Virginia Company, their Treasurer, or any two of the Council, were empowered to adminster the Oaths of Supremacy, and of Allegiance, to all persons going to their Colony. And the Pilgrims, through their chief men, agreed with the Virginia Company: "The Oath of Supremacy we shall willingly take, if it be required of us, if that convenient satisfaction be not given by our taking the Oath of Allegiance. John Robinson. William Brewster."

The Charter of the Massachusetts-Bay Company gave them broader powers in that it did not exact this provision from them but gave the Company liberty to admit new members, called "Freemen" of the Company, and no method, conditions, or qualifications were presented for conferring this privilege. Their leaders, as we shall see, were quick to take advantage of the opportunity given them to frame their own Oaths of citizenship. Too late the government in England, or rather that part which was representative of the Church of England, realized the powers of colonization this gave the dissenting churchmen; and, in 1637, a Proclamation was issued, aimed principally to prevent the emigration of Puritan Ministers, which commanded that none should be suffered to go to New England "without a certificate that they had taken the Oaths of Supremacy and Allegiance, and had conformed to the discipline of the Church of England." In 1638, another Proclamation "commanded owners and masters of vessels that they do not fit out any with passengers and provisions to New-England, without license from the Commissioners of Plantations."

Another Oath, drawn up in England, also claims a place here because it was sometimes voluntarily taken by settlers in the New England Colonies. In the year 1655, during the Protectorate of Oliver Cromwell, an Oath, probably similar to that prescribed by the Rump Parliament to the Council of State, was enacted which was known as:

THE OATH OF ABJURATION

I do hereby swear that I do renounce the pretended title of Charles Stuart, and the whole line of the late King James; and of any other person, as a single person pretending, or which shall pretend to the crown or government of these nations of England Scotland and Ireland, or any of them; and that I will, by the grace and assistance of Almighty God, be true, faithful and constant to the Parliament, and Commonwealth; and will oppose the bringing in, or setting up any single person or House of Lords, and every   of them, in this Commonwealth.

Soon after the Restoration, Charles the Second, by Proclamation commanded that the Oaths of Supremacy and Allegiance be tendered to all persons disaffected to the Government and, in case of refusal, that they were to be prosecuted under the Statute of the 7th of James. During the reign of his Roman Catholic successor, James the Second, the Oath of Supremacy was allowed to lapse, and the Oath of Allegiance, only, was in full force in the Colonies, up to the publication of his declaration of liberty of conscience for all denominations in England and Scotland, in 1687-1688, which sealed his doom.

These preliminaries are necessary to a full understanding of our subject which naturally begins, in point of time, with the settlement

In New Plymouth Colony.

Strictly speaking, Plymouth was not a New England Colony. It was without a Charter, and the functions of its government were those of a Corporation. The power of the Oath of Allegiance their leaders had assented to always seemed to hang over them, and paralyze the initiative they should have taken. Their attempts to increase their circumscribed boundaries at New Plymouth were futile; and, in the case of their attempted settlement in Maine, disastrous both to the business reputation of their leaders, and to the Corporation. They could spare neither the men nor the means from the parent settlement to form permanent settlements elsewhere. They seemed doomed to failure. And yet hardly that, when we consider the impress upon our Nation made by their sterling qualities of mind and heart, their patience and fortitude under severe trials, the hopes and ambition of their teachings, and their never-failing trust in God's Providence. These high qualities still animate and live in the great and growing number who proudly claim their ancestry from the Pilgrims at New Plymouth.

COMBINATION FOR FOUNDATION OF GOVERNMENT
known as
THE MAYFLOWER COMPACT

In y° name of God, Amen. We whose names are underwriten, the loyall subjects of our dread soveraigne Lord, King James, by y° grace of God, of Great Britaine, Franc, & Ireland, king, defender of y° faith, &c. haveing undertaken, for y° glorie of God, and advancement of y° Christian faith, and honour of our king and countrie, a voyage to plant y° first colonie in y° Northerne parts of Virginia, doe by these presents solemnly & mutualy in y° presence of God, and one of another, covenant & combine our selves togeather into a civill body politick, for our better ordering & preservation & furtherance of y° ends aforesaid; and by vertue hearof to enacte, constitute, and frame such just & equall lawes, ordinances, acts, constitutions, & offices, from time to time, as shall be thought most meete & convenient for y° generall good of y° Colonie, unto which we promise all due submission and obedience. In witnes wherof we have hereunder subscribed our names at Cap-Codd y° 11 of November, in y° year of y° raigne of our soveraigne lord, King James, of England, France, & Ireland y° eighteenth, and of Scotland y° fiftie fourth. An°: Dom. 1620. [Forty-one names.]

The Mayflower Compact has received full and adequate treatment in the paper read before this Society in October, 1920, by Arthur Lord, LL.D.

The exact date of the two forms of Oaths first given has not been determined, but they are certainly later than the formation of the first Council in 1624.

Oath of Allegiance and Fidelity

The forme of Oath . . . . . which liue in this Colonie
. . . . the Oth of alegance to his maj . .
fidelity to the same.

You shall sweare by the name of the Great God . . . . & earth & in his holy fear, & presence that you shall not speake, or doe, deuise, or aduise, anything or things, acte or acts, directly, or indirectly, By land, or water, that doth, shall, or may, tend to the destruction or ouerthrowe of this present plantation, Colonie, or Corporation of this towne Plimouth in New England.

Neither shall you suffer the same to be spoken, or done, but shall hinder, & oposse the same, by all due means you can.

You shall not enter into any league, treaty, Confederac̄ or combination, with any, within the said Colonie or without the same that shall plote, or contriue any thing to the hurte, & ruine of the growth, and good of the said plantation.

You shall not consente to any shuch confederation, nor conceale any known vnto you certainly, or by conje· but shall forthwith manifest & make knowne the same, to the Gouernours of this said towne for the time being.

And this you promise & swear, simply, & truly, & faithfully to performe as a true christian [you hope for help from God, the God of truth & punisher of falshoode.]

The forme of the Oath which . . . . . . of the Gouernour, & Counsell at euery Election of any of them.

You shall swear, according to that wisdom, and measure of discerning giuen vnto you; faithfully, equally & indifrently without respect of persons; to administer Justice, in all causes coming before you. And shall labor, to aduance, & furder the good of this Colony, & plantation, to the vtmost of your power; and oppose any thing that may hinder the same. So help you God.

The words, "a true christian" were afterwards crossed out, and the form used later: "as you hope for help from God, the God of truth and punisher of falsehood" was substituted.

By the Laws of 1636, every freeman was required to take the following Oath:

THE OATH OF A FFREEMAN

You shall be truly loyall to our Sov Lord King Charles, his heires & successors. [the State & Govern^t of England as it now stands.] You shall not speake or doe, devise or advise any thing or things act or acts directly or indirectly by land or water, that doth shall or may tend to the destrucõon or overthrow of this prnt plantaõons Colonies or Corporaõon of New Plymouth, Neither shall you suffer the same to be spoken or done but shall hinder oppose & discover the same to the Govr̄ & Assistants of the said Colony for the time being or some one of them. You shall faithfully submit unto such good & wholesome laws & ordnanc & as either are or shall be made for the ordering & governm^t of the same, and shall endeavor to advance the growth & good of the severall Colonies plantations wth in the limit & of this Corporaõon by all due meanes & courses. All wch you promise & sweare by the name of the great God of heaven & earth simply truly & faithfully to pforme as you hope for help frō God who is the God of truth & punisher of falsehood. [1636]

Following the outbreak of civil war in England in 1638, the words "our sovereign lord King Charles his heirs and successors" were erased, and loyalty to "the State and Government of England as it now stands" substituted. The modern rendering intermixed is probably an attempt by the transcriber to fill out missing or undecipherable paragraphs or sentences.

According to Francis Baylies' "Historical Memoir of New Plymouth," (I: 235,) the following Oath was prescribed to be taken by any residing in the government of New Plymouth:

THE OATH OF A RESIDENT

You shall be truly loyal to our sovereign lord King Charles, his heirs and successors, and whereas you choose at present to reside within the government of New Plymouth, you shall not do or cause to be done any act or acts directly or indirectly, by land or water, that shall tend to the destruction or overthrow of the whole or any of the several plantations or townships within the said government that are or shall be orderly erected or established, but shall contrariwise hinder, oppose, and discover the same, and such intents and purposes as tend thereunto, to the Governor for the time being, or some one of the assistants with all convenient speed. You shall also submit unto and obey all such good and wholesome laws, ordinances, and offices as are or shall be established within the limits thereof. So help you God. [1636.]

The disturbed state of England is also reflected in the 1658 revision of the Laws when "our sovereign lord the King, his heirs and successors" is substituted for "the present State and Government of England," as follows:

THE OATH OF A FFREEMAN

You shalbee truely Loyall to the present State and Goūment of England [our Sou^r Lord the King his heires and Successors.] You shall not speake or doe deuise or aduise Any thinge or thinges Acte or Actes directly or Indirectly by Land or Water that doth shall or may tend to the destruction or ouerthrow of these present plantations or Townshipes of the Corporation of New Plymouth neither shall you suffer the same to bee spoken or done but shall hinder oppose and discouer the same to the Gou^r And Assistants of the said Collonie for the time being; or some one of them; you shall faithfully submitt vnto such good and wholesome Lawes and ordinances as either are or shalbee made for the ordering and Gou^{r}ment of the same; and shall Indeuor to aduance the grouth and good of the seuerall townshipes and plantations within the Lymetts of this Corporation by all due meanes and courses; All which you pmise and Sweare by the Name of the great God of heauen and earth simply truely and faithfully to pforme as you hope for healp from God who is the God of truth and the punisher of falchood. [1658.]

At the time of the 1671 revision of the Laws, Charles the Second had been firmly seated on the English throne for ten years, but his name is omitted from the superscription of the following Oath. The intensity of the feeling in the New England Colonies towards even the name of the two kings is shown in the fact that until after the middle of the next century Harvard College had only three graduates, if the three Charles Chaunceys, with whom it was a family name in England, are omitted, and Yale College only one graduate who bore the Christian name of Charles.

12

THE OATH OF A FFREEMAN

You shalbee truely Loyall to our Sou^r Lord the Kinge his heires and Successors; you shall not doe nor speake deuise or aduise any thinge or thinges act or actes directly or Inderectly by Land or water; that shall or may tend to the destruction or ouerthrow of any of these plantations or towneshipes of the Corporation of New Plymouth; neither shall you suffer the same to bee spoken or done but shall hinder oppose and discouer the same to the Gou^r and Assistants of the said Collonie for the time being or some one of them; you shall faithfully submitt vnto such good and wholesome lawes and ordinances; as either are or shalbee made for the ordering and Gou^rment of the same; and shall endeauor to advance the good and grouth of the seuerall Towneshipes and plantations within the Lymetts of this Corporation by all due meanes and courses; all which you p^rmise and sweare by the Name of the great God of heauen and earth simply truely and faithfully to pforme as you hope for healpe from God whoe is the God of truth and the punisher of ffalchood. [1671.]

In Massachusetts-Bay Colony.

When on the 4th of March 1628/9, Charles, "by the grace of God, Kinge of England, Scotland, Fraunce, and Ireland, Defender of the Fayth, &c. in the fourth yeare of our raigne" did by letters patent grant unto Sir Henry Rosewell and his twenty-five associates, their heirs and assigns forever, all that certain part of the grant of New England which his "deare and royall father, Kinge James of blessed memory . . . hath given and graunted vnto the Counsell established at Plymouth in the County of Devon" and which the said Council by deed dated the 19th of March, 1627/8, had "given, graunted, bargained, soulde, enfeoffed, aliened and confirmed" to Sir Henry Rosewell, Sir John Young, Knightes, Thomas Southcott, John Humphrey, John Endecott and Symon Whetcombe, their heirs and associates forever, To be houlden of vs our heires and successors, as of our manor of East-greenewich, in the County of Kent, within our realme of England," under the name of the "Governor and Company of the Mattachusetts Bay in Newe England, one bodie politique and corporate in deede, fact, and name, . . . and that by that name they shall have perpetuall succession,"—may acquire lands, &c. have a common seal; and that there shall be one Governor, one Deputy Governor, and eighteen assistants to be chosen out of the freemen. He went farther, and constituted "our welbeloved Mathewe Cradocke to be the first and present Governor; Thomas Goffe to be Deputy Governor, and eighteen of the other associates to be Assistants, who before they undertake the execution of their offices and places shall respectively take their corporal oaths for the faithful performance of their duties. The Oath for Matthew Craddock, as Governor, to be administered by a Master of the Chancery, the Governor was then empowered to administer the oaths to the Deputy Governor and Assistants nominated in the Charter. Oaths to subsequent officers being arranged: the new Governor to take the Oath before the old Deputy Governor, or two Assistants; and the new Deputy Governor, Assistants and all other officers hereafter chosen to take the oath before the Governor for the time being. They were empowered to transport any of our loving subjects, or any strangers willing to become our loving subjects, and any seven at least of their number had "full power and authoritie to choose, nominate, and appointe such and soe many others as they shall thinke fitt, and that shall be willing to accept the same, to be free of the said Company and Body, and Them into the same to admitt." All subjects inhabiting the lands granted, and their children "which shall happen to be borne there, or on the seas in goeing thither, or retorning from thence shall have and enjoy all liberties and immunities of free and natural subjects, . . . as yf they and everie of them were borne within the realme of England." And the Governor and Deputy Governor, and any two or more of the Assistants, at any of their Courts or Assemblys shall and may at all times have full power to give the Oath of Office and Oaths of

Supremacy and Allegiance, or either of them, to every
person who may go to New England to inhabit in the
same. They were also authorized to make "the
formes of such Oathes warrantable by the lawes and
statutes of this our realme of England as shalbe res-
pectivelie ministered vnto them, for the execuŏon of
the said severall offices and places . . . and ministr-
ing the said oathes to the newe elected officers."

At the end of the Charter appeared the Oath of
Governor:

PRÆDICT, Matthaeus Cradocke Juratus est de Fide et
Obedientiâ Regi et Successoribus suis, et de Debitâ Exequutione
Officij Gubernatoris iuxta Tenorem P^r sentium, 18° Martij,
1628. Coram me, Carola Cæsare, Milite, in Cancellariâ Mŕo.

Char. Cæsar.

By this Charter, under the privy seal of Cardinal
Wolseley, was, unwittingly, planted the seed of the
fairest flower that ever bloomed in the garden of
colonization since Eden.

Up to August, 1630, the business of the Massachusetts-Bay Company was transacted in London.
But the business of the Massachusetts-Bay Colony
may be said to have really begun in May, 1631.

At "A Gen^rall Court holden att Boston, the 18th
day of May, 1631. John Winthrop, Esq was chosen
Goun^r for a whole yeare nexte ensueinge by the
gen^rall consent of the Court, according to the meaneing
of the pattent, and did accordingly take an oathe to
the place of Goun^r belonginge."

"Tho: Dudley, Esq, is also chosen Deputy
Goun^r for this yeare nexte ensuing, & did in p^rsence of
the Court take an oath to his place belonginge."

And "to the end the body of the comons may be
p^rserued of honest & good men, it was likewise ordered
and agreed that for time to come noe man shalbe
admitted to the freedome of this body polliticke, but
such as are members of some of the churches within
the lymitts of the same."

The Law that all freemen must be church members, while assented to in Salem in 1631, was modified in 1632, probably for local reasons, that no civil magistrate could be an elder in the church.

To give force to this law an Oath of Freemen was required, and this service the newly appointed Governor and the Deputy Governor elected to perform. The result of their labors, the original draft of the Oath of a Freeman, in the handwriting of the first and greatest of the Governors of the Commonwealth of Massachusetts, and the Oath of a Servant, in the handwriting of the second Governor—a document perhaps only surpassed in historical interest and importance by, and worthy to rank with, the Declaration of Independence—is now, appropriately, in the possession of the Public Library of the City of Boston, and its preservation assured.

Through the courtesy of the Trustees, this Society is permitted again to give publicity to the excellent facsimiles of these interesting documents, together with transcriptions of the somewhat obscure handwriting, with interlineations and cancelled words showing, line for line, the changes made by the authors, which first appeared in the *Bulletin* of the Library for July, 1894.

THE OATH OF A FREEMAN, OR OF A MAN TO BE MADE FFREE.

I, A. B. &c. being, by the Almighties most wise disposicon, become a memb^r of this body, consisting of the Goūn^r, Deputy Goūn^r, Assistants, & a com^{n}lty of the Mattachusets in Newe England, doe, freely & sincerely acknowledge that I am iustly & lawfully subject to the goūm^t of the same, & doe accordingly submitt my pson & estate to be ptected, ordered, & goūned by the lawes & constitucons thereof, & doe faithfully pmise to be from time to time obedient & conformeable therevnto, & to the authie of the said Goūn^r & Assistants & their success^{r}s, & to all such lawes, orders, sentences, & decrees as shalbe lawfully made & published by them or their successors; and I will alwaies indeav^r (as in dutie I am bound) to advance the peace & wellfaire of this bodie or comonwealth to my vtmost skill & abilitie; & I will, to my best power & meanes, seeke to devert & prevent whatsoeuer may tend to the ruyne or damage thereof, or of any the said Goūn^r, Deputy Goūn^r, or Assistants, or any of them, or

The oath of a serv[t].

I. N. N. serv[t] of &c. haveinge heard and vnderstoode that our —
soveraigne Lord Kinge Charles hath by his łres patents vnder the
great seale of England graunted power and aucthoryty vnto
a Governo[r] a Deputy Governo[r] &. 18. Assistants to rule governe
& Judge all psones wch doe or shall inhabyte in or betweene
the Charles ryver &. 3. myles southward & merimack ryver
&. 3. myles northwards in new England & soe westwards to
the south sea, beinge wthin wch compa lymitts I doe nowe —
inhabyt

Doe promise to be at all tymes hereafter Dureinge my abode
    to. be
in America obedyent to all lawes orders constitutions &
    ^
comaunds wch by the s b said Governo[r] Deputy Governo[r] and
  for the tyme being   lawfully
assistants or the greater pte of them shall be made or given —
  ^   ^
forth & shall come to my k heareinge, And to be true and faith
full to them & their governemt, And I likewise promise that if I
  heare of or heare of or suspect
shall know of any hurt or losse intended against any of them I will
  ^
reveale the same to one or more of them wth all convenyent —
speede, And to bind my selfe to the faithfull pformance of this
promise, I sweare by the name of the onely true God the lover of
truth & the avenger of falshood

Fac-simile of the Freemen's Oath

free or
The oath of a man to be made free.
^

being
I. N. N. vt supra, and having likewice heard and vnderstoode
I ye said. N. N. of being now by the said Governor & assistants to be made a free
thereby enabled
man of the said plantacon & to have a voice in the choise of
^
the said. 20. Deputed psones soe aucthorised as aforesaid as the
sai any of their places are or shalbe voide and I shalbe therevnto
called in a lawfull assembly, doe hereby promice vt supra
I doe promise that when I s at all tymes when I shalbe there
vnto lawfully called by the said Governemt, to give my voice
for the electing of such psone therevnto & psones vnto such voide
places as I the shall und thinke to be the wiseet godliest
& ablest for the discharg men of wisedome & courage —
feareinge God & hateing covetousnes all ptyalyty & by sett
aside, and to bind &c vt supra.

The Oath of ffreemen:

1 A: B: &c: beinge beinge by the Allmightyes most wise desposĩtio become
a member of this bodye consisting of the Governor Deputye Assistants & Comõnalty
of the Mattachusetts in n: e: doe freely & sincerely acknowledge that I
am iustlye & lawfully subiect to the Goverment both Civill & Ecclesiasticall there of the same & doe
accordingly submitt my pson & estate to be protected ordered & governed
by the Lawes & Constitutns therof: & doe faithfully promise to be
from tyme to tyme obedient & conformable therevnto, & to the Authe of the
sd Governor & Assistants & their successors, & to all such Lawes orders
sentences & decrees as shalbe made lawfully & published by them or their successors
And I will allwayes endeavoᵣ (as in dutye I am bounde) to advance the
peace & wellfare of this bodye or Com: w: to my vttmost power & skill & ability.
And I will to my vtmost power best ability power & meanes seeke to de-
verte & prevent whatsoever may tende to the ruyne or damage thereof
or of any the sd Governor Deputy Governor or Assistants or any of them
or their successors: & will give spedye notice to them or some of them of
any evill seditio, violence, treacherye or other hurt or evill, wch I shall
knowe, heare, or vehemently suspecte to be intended or plotted or intended
agᵗ them sd or agᵗ the said Goverment Com: w: or the sd Goverm̃
established:
And I will not at any tyme suffer or give Consent to any Counsell
or Attempt that shalbe offered or given or Attempted for the impeachment
of the sd Goverment or makinge any change or Alteratio of the same, contrary
to the Lawes & Customes ordinances of the same thereof, but shall doe my
vtmost endeavoᵣ to discover & oppose & hier all & everye such Counsells
& Attempts   F.

their success^{r}s, and will giue speedy notice to them, or some of them, of any sediĉon, violence, treachery, or other hurt or euill which I shall knowe, heare, or vehem^{t}ly suspecte to be plotted or intended against the said coṁonwealth, or the said goum^t established; and I will not att any time suffer or giue consent to any counsell or attempt that shalbe offered giuen, or attempted for the impeachm^t of the said goūm^t, or makeing any change or alteraĉon of the same, contrary to the lawes & ordinances thereof, but shall doe my vtmost endeav^r to discover, oppose, & hinder, all & eūy such counsell & attempts. Soe helpe me God. [1631.]

Att a Gen^{r}all Court, holden att Newe Towne [Cambridge]. March 4th, 1634.

It is further ordered that eūy man of or above the age of sixteene yeares, whoe hath bene, or shall hereafter be, resident within this iurisdicĉon by the space of sixe monethes, (as well servants as others,) & not infranchized, shall take the oath of residents before the Goūn^r, Deputy Goūn^r, or two of the nexte Assistants, whoe shall haue power to convent him for that purpose, & vpon his refuseall, to binde him ouer to the nexte Court of Assistants, & vpon his refuseall the second tyme, to be punished att the discreĉon of the Court.

It is ordered that the ffreemens oath shalbe gyven to eūy man of or above the age of 16 yeares, the clause for the elecĉon of magistrates onely excepted.

At A Court holden att Boston, Aprill 1th, 1634.

It was further ordered, that eūy man of or above the age of twenty yeares, whoe hath bene or shall hereafter be resident within this jurisdicĉon by the space of sixe monethes, as an householder or soiorner, and not infranchised, shall take the oath herevnder written, before the Goūn^r, or Deputy Goūn^r, or some two of the nexte Assistants, whoe shall haue power to convent him for that purpose, and vpon his refuseall, to binde him ouer to the nexte Court of Assistants; and vpon his refuseall the second tyme, hee shalbe banished, except the Court shall see cause to giue him further respite.

THE OATH OF RESIDENTS

I doe heare sweare, and call God to witnes, that, being nowe an inhabitant within the lymitts of this juridicĉon of the Massachusetts, I doe acknowledge myselfe lawfully subject to the aucthoritie and gouerm^t there established, and doe accordingly submitt my pson, family, and estate, to be ptected, ordered, & gouerned by the lawes & constituĉons thereof, and doe faithfully pmise to be from time to time obedient and conformeable therevnto, and to the aucthoritie of the Goūn^r, and all other the Magistrates there, and their success^rs, and to all such lawes, orders, sentences, & decrees, as nowe are or hereafter shalbe lawfully made, decreed, & published by them or their success^rs. And I will alwayes indeav^r (as in duty I am bound) to advance the peace & wellfaire of this body pollitique, and I will (to my best power & meanes) seeke to devert & prevent whatsoeuer may tende to the ruine or damage thereof, or of ye Goūn^r, Deputy Goūn^r, or Assistants, or any of them or their success^rs, and will giue speedy notice to them, or some of them, of any sedicōn, violence, treacherie, or oth^r hurte or euill wch I shall knowe, heare, or vehemently suspect to be plotted or intended against them or any of them, or against the said Comōn-wealth or goum^t established. Soe helpe mee God. [1634.]

Att a Gen^rall Courte, holden att Boston, May 14th, 1634.
It was agreed & ordered, that the former oath of ffreemen shalbe revoked, soe farr as it is dissonant from the oath of ffreemen herevnder written, & that those that receaved the former oath shall stand bound noe further thereby, to any intent or purpose, then this newe oath tyes those that nowe takes ye same.

THE OATH OF A FREEMAN

I, A. B., being, by Gods providence, an inhabitant & ffreeman within the jurisdiccōn of this comōnweale, doe freely acknowledge my selfe to be subiect to the goverm^t thereof, & therefore doe heere sweare, by the greate & dreadfull name of the euerlyveing God, that I wilbe true & faithfull to the same, & will accordingly yeilde assistance & support therevnto, with my pson & estate, as in equity I am bound, & will also truely indeav^r to mainetaine & preserue all the libertyes & previlidges thereof, submitting my selfe to the wholesome lawes & orders made & established by the same; and furth^r, that I will not plott nor practise any evill against it, nor consent to any that shall soe doe, but will timely discover & reveale the same to lawfull aucthority nowe here established, for the speedy preventing thereof. Moreouer, I doe solemnely binde myselfe, in the sight of God, that when I shalbe called to giue my voice touching any such matter of this state, wherein ffreemen are to deale I will giue my vote & suffrage, as I shall iudge in myne owne conscience may best conduce & tend to the publique weale of the body, without respect of psons, or fav^r of any man. Soe helpe mee God in the Lord Jesus Christ. [1634.]
Further, it is agreed that none but the Geñ all Court hath power to chuse and admitt freemen.

The text of the Oath given above is that given in the body of the Colony Records, in the handwriting of Simon Bradstreet, the Secretary, and differs only in the spelling of words from that of the transcriber (who may have been Secretary Bradstreet himself) of the copy in the Miscellaneous Records, which were transferred by the Compiler from their regular order to the end of the first volume of the Records at page 354.

THE OATH OF A FREE-MAN

I (A. B.) being by Gods providence an Inhabitant, and Freeman, within the Jurisdiction of this Commonwealth; do freely acknowledge my self to be subject to the Government thereof: And therefore do here swear by the great and dreadful Name of the Ever-living God, that *I* will be true and faithfull to the same, and will accordingly yield assistance & support thereunto, with my person and estate, as in equity *I* am bound; and will also truly endeavour to maintain and preserve all the liberties and priviledges thereof, submitting my self to the wholesome Lawes & Orders made and established by the same. And further that *I* will not plot or practice any evill against it, or consent to any that shall so do; but will timely discover and reveal the same to lawfull Authority now here established, for the speedy preventing thereof. Moreover, *I* doe solemnly bind my self in the sight of God, that when *I* shal be called to give my voyce touching any such matter of this State, in which Freemen are to deal, *I* will give my vote and suffrage as *I* shall judge in mine own conscience may best conduce and tend to the publike weal of the body, without respect of persons, or favour of any man. So help me God in the Lord Jesus Christ. [1634.] From the copy given in John Childe's "New-Englands Jonas cast up at London." (London, 1647), which the preface states was printed in Massachusetts-Bay, by itself.

To this form of The Oath of a Free man attaches the great additional interest of being the first work printed in the United States of America.

Under date of Mo. 1. (March, 1638/9) John Winthrop's Journal states: "A printing house was begun at Cambridge by one Daye, at the charge of Mr. Glover, who died on sea hitherward. The first thing which was printed was the freemen's oath; the next was an almanac made for New England by Mr.

William Peirce, mariner; the next was the Psalms newly turned into metre."

For nearly three hundred years no copy of this printed paper has been known to be extant. The ceaseless search for a copy in this country by antiquarians, bibliographers and historians would long ago have been successful, if even a single copy had been preserved in either the institutions of the State, or Nation, or in individual or family possession.

It would be difficult to exaggerate the patriotic feeling of our people, if it were known that a copy of this interesting and valuable state paper, the first fruit of the printing-press in this country, whose ringing sentences of freedom preceded by nearly a century and a half the Declaration of Independence, had been discovered at this late day.

Fully a quarter of a century ago, while engaged in making a search for early printed American publications in the Catalogue of printed books in the British Museum—a great and monumental work, worthy in its scholarly completeness of the Government which fostered its publication, and of inestimable importance and benefit to scholars in every land—the following entry under the heading "Freeman" seemed to me to warrant more than passing observation and curiosity which the intervening years have failed to satisfy:

—The Oath of a Freeman. B. L.
[*London*, 1645?] *s. sh.* 12°. 11,626. aa. (1, 2.)

An analysis of this entry seems to show points of resemblance following closely the known facts regarding the first work printed in this country.

The title is the one given by John Childe presumably from the earliest printed copy in his possession. The abbreviated title, freemen's oath, as given by John Winthrop, first appearing in the Code of 1648, which seems to justify the belief that Winthrop wrote his Journal some years after the press was established.

The letters B. L. indicate that the printed text is in black-letter. While there is no evidence of the number and kinds of fonts of type purchased for the first press by Joseph Glover, there is an itemized statement of the number and names of the fonts of type for the second press sent over later by the Society for Propagating the Gospel among the Indians in New England, for printing the Bible in the Indian language, and among them is a small font of "blacks," i.e. black-letter, which would indicate that a small font of that letter was generally considered a part of the equipment of a printing-office of the period. Even if this was not so, on the good authority of Isaiah Thomas, the type used in printing the Bay Psalm Book, of 1640, was "small bodied English," a type commonly used for works in quarto and folio, which approximates in size to black-letter, but without the ceriphs, or fine projecting points of that letter. It is not unreasonable to suppose that a cataloguer might, hastily, consider the thickly inked, heavy press-work we find in the Bay Psalm Book, under the same conditions in a somewhat crudely printed sheet, to be black-letter printing.

The brackets enclosing the imprint indicate that the place and date given do not appear on the printed sheet, but are the personal judgment of the cataloguer regarding them. Having already determined the printing to be in black-letter English, it naturally follows in his judgment that the place of printing is London. His guess of the year, 1645, which he queries, is a close one; but is open to the criticism that an Oath of a Freeman could never have been printed or exacted in England during the reign of Charles the First. Ten years later, under Cromwellian rule, it might have been done. But the only place on earth it could have been printed and exacted without imprisonment, in 1645, was in the freemen's Colony of Massachusetts-Bay.

In this connection it may be well to observe, as a further illustration that Governor Winthrop wrote his

Journal years later than the events he records, that his date of 1638/9, should be one year later, for the date of the half-sheet almanac by William Peirce, mariner. Following Winthrop, if the almanac was calculated for the year beginning in March, 1639, it would suppose its printing sometime before the 25th of March, or in the Julian year 1638. This would leave nearly a whole year during which no other printing was done. If the almanac was calculated for the year beginning in March, 1640—the year the Bay Psalm Book is dated—then it would suppose the Oath, and the Almanac, printed in the eleventh or twelfth months of the Julian year 1639, which is more probable. Isaiah Thomas, writing in 1810, leaves this question in doubt by not stating whether his January, 1639, refers to the Julian, or the Gregorian Calendar.

To continue our analysis: The format, and size, agrees with the known facts that the Oath was printed "on the face of a half sheet of small paper." The shelf-mark indicates the permanent place on the shelves of the Library.

The singular appearance of the only known copy of this important and interesting document in the Colonial history of New England, nearly three hundred years after its printing, so far from its place of publication, calls for explanation, which is apparently furnished in a work published in London, in April, 1647, entitled: "New-Englands Jonas cast up at London." On the title-page it purports to be written by Major John Childe, a brother of Doctor Robert Childe, of Hingham, who was detained by order of the General Court of Massachusetts-Bay; but according to William Hubbard, in his History, and affirmed by John Winthrop, in his Journal, the real author of everything, except the Preface, was William Vassall.

Its odd title was suggested by a remark made by the Reverend John Cotton, in a Thursday-Lecture, preached November 5, 1646, just previous to the departure of the vessel which was carrying back to

England some of the dissatisfied signers of a Petition to the General Court, who rumor gave were taking with them this and other incriminating documents against the Government of the Colony. The learned preacher took for his text, Canticles, II: 15. "Take us the foxes, the little foxes, which destroy the vines," and made pointed allusions to the current rumors, and the punishment which their acts would receive in a stormy voyage, and how it could be averted. But later we shall let Vassall tell the story in his own words. The effect upon his hearers was so great that some who had engaged passage withdrew rather than risk the dangers of a stormy voyage in the winter season.

After a brief summary of the reasons for publication the Preface states that the Relation is made up of the following particulars:

First, the Petition of the greater part of the Inhabitants of Hingham, and the proceedings therein.

Secondly, a Petition of Doctor Child and others delivered to the General Court at Boston with some passages thereon.

Thirdly, the Capital Laws of the Massachusetts Bay, with the Freemans Oath, *as they are printed there by themselves.*

The italics are mine. Here, then, we have direct proof confirming the statement of John Winthrop that the Freeman's Oath was printed at Cambridge in 1639, and, in the body of the work, is given the full text of The Oath of a Free man as printed. It is probable that only the number of copies necessary for officials authorized to administer the Oath were printed, and the copy taken to England was surreptitiously obtained from some member of the Government. Its importance lay in the fact that it afforded printed evidence that nowhere in it is any reference made to the King's Majesty, or of allegiance to any power on earth save that of their own Government as constituted.

The Capital Laws were printed at Cambridge in 1642, probably under the same restriction, as to num-

ber; and, as printed evidence, open to the same
construction as the Oath. Whatever the purpose,
however, it had been forestalled some four years
earlier when the Capital Laws were reprinted in London in a folio broadside. The copy in the British
Museum bears the Colophon: "Printed first in New-
England, and re-printed in London for Ben. Allen in
Popes-Head Allen [*sic*] 1643."

Fourthly, a relation of that story of Jonas verbatim as it
was delivered to me in writing by a Gentleman that was then
a passenger in the ship.

"When the first ship that came this year 1646 from New-
England, was almost ready to come from thence; Mr.
Cotton in his Thursday-Lecture at Boston, preached out of
that Scripture, Cant. 2, 15. Take us the little Foxes, &c.
In his uses took occasion to say, That if any shall carry any
Writings, Complaints against the people of God in that
Country it would be a Jonas in the ship. * * He also
advised the Ship-Master, that if storms did arise, to search if
they had not in any Chest or Trunk any such Jonas aboard,
which if you find (said he) I do not advise you to throw the
persons over-board, but the Writings; or words to that effect.
Whereupon, having great storms (as could not be otherwise
expected) some of the Passengers remembering Mr. Cotton's
Sermon, it seems were much affected with what he had said;
and a woman amongst them came up from between the decks
about Midnight, or after, in a distracted passionate manner to
Mr. William Vassall who lay in the great Cabin, but for the
present was in the Sterage-door-way looking abroad: she
earnestly desired him, if there were any Jonas in the ship, that
as Mr. Cotton had directed it might be thrown over-board,
with many broken expressions to that purpose. He asked
her why she came to him? and she said because it was thought
that he had some Writings against the people of God: but
he answered her, He had nothing but a Petition to the
Parliament that they might enjoy the liberty of English subjects, and that could be no Jonas; and that if the best of New-
Englands friends could shew him any evil in that, he would not
prefer it. After this she went into the great Cabin to Mr.
Tho. Fowle in like distracted manner; who told her he had
nothing but the Copy of Petition which himself and others had
presented to the Court at Boston; and showed, and read it to
her, and then told her, That if she and others thought that to
be the cause of the storm, she and they might do what they

would with it; but he professed that he saw no evil in it, neither was his Conscience troubled with it. So she took it and carried it between Decks to them from whom she came, and they agreed to throw it over-board and it was thrown over-board: but the storm did not leave us upon the throwing of the Paper over-board as it is reported; for they had many great storms after that; much lesse was the great and wonderfull deliverance which by Gods mercy he gave unto them from shipwrack and drowning at the Isles of Silly, upon the throwing of that Writing over-board; for that was thrown over long before, at least 14 dayes. Also the error is the more in this, That the report is that it was the petition to the Parliament that was thrown over-board; and it was only a Copy of a Petition to their own Court at Boston, and the Petition to the Parliament was still in the ship, together with another copy of that which was thrown over-board, and other writings of that nature, some of which are printed in this book, and were as well saved as their lives and other goods, and are here in London to be seen and made use of in convenient time."

It is true that at any time in the intervening years of a quarter of a century I could have written to the British Museum authorities and been sure of a courteous reply; but the matter seemed too important to be settled in so prosaic a way. This, and the hope that sometime I might be able to determine the matter personally, and achieve the honor that would attach to its discovery, deterred me.

I suppose that men of all professions, in their callings, feel an unwonted glow in the achievement of some object; but I know of no greater joy than that which fills the lover of books when his long search for a rare book is rewarded. Then it is that you seem to enter into the holy of holies of delight, when the whole body thrills with suppressed emotions, the eyes moisten, and the trembling hand stretched out to take the volume does so with a touch which is almost a caress. The feeling, I think, must be somewhat akin to the "buck fever" of the deer hunter, whose mind and shaking limbs refuse to function, as he looks into the luminous eyes, and notes the startled look, and graceful beauty of his prey, until it has bounded into safety in the forest. Why, I reasoned with myself, should I give to another the pleasure of these emotions which were mine by right of discovery.

The opportunity of voyaging to England, which I had so long looked forward to, did not come to me until the Spring of the present year, and the pleasant anticipations with which I set out were comparable in my own mind with those which must have animated the Knights of Arthur's Round Table in their quest for the holy grail. The morning after my arrival in London found me an early visitor at the British Museum. The preliminaries of admittance to the Reading-Room are not difficult, and are soon over with, and I found myself within the great rotunda, its walls lined in tiers with what is best in the literatures of the world, and from which has gone out so much that is worth while in English literature. From the Catalogue I filled out slips for some half dozen works, artfully to conceal the one uppermost in my mind, handed them in at the desk, and returned to my chosen seat to await with such calmness as I could command the culmination of years of desire. Heeding the legend that when the grail was approached by any one not perfectly pure it vanished from sight; and that to be qualified to discover it one must be perfectly chaste in thought and act, I endeavored to prepare myself for its appearance. Somewhere I have read of an Oriental visionary who attained a high degree of saintly perfection by fixing his gaze steadfastly for hours upon his navel, which a growing embonpoint made an easy thing to do, and I sought for holiness in the same way.

In time the white slips of my wants came fluttering back to me by messengers, all marked, very properly for security on account of rarity, that they could only be consulted in the North Library, until all were in but the one most desired. Then followed a much longer wait and then— the slip was handed back to me with a notation that I had given a wrong shelf-mark! Gone in an instant were all the perfectly pure and chaste thoughts with which I had been regaling myself while I was apparently looking at the wrong button on my vest. I think I could have stood the blow better if it had been that hoary old fiction of careless assistants that it was "out", but this is a boon denied to any assistant in the British Museum, where nothing is allowed to go out. A comparison with the printed Catalogue showed an exact correspondence, and I sought the Superintendent of the Reading-Room, who assured me that the matter would have his personal attention; and for the rest of the day I busied myself with my other wants in the North Library without any word of the missing broadside reaching me. That evening, in communion with myself, I determined to throw off the mask of secrecy and frankly confide the importance of my quest to the Keeper of the Printed Books—the somewhat expressive and imposing title of the Librarian of the British Musuem.

Before calling upon him I sought as an introducer Henry N. Stevens—the worthy son of an illustrious father who follows closely in his footsteps as the best authority on early printed American books in Europe—at his shop across the street from the imposing Museum building, and to him I told my story. As I proceeded his interest grew, and before I had finished he excitedly grasped my arm with one hand and his hat with the other, exclaiming: "Come with me. This is not a subject for underlings," and rushed me across the street without pause until we were in the sanctum sanctorum of the learned and accomplished Keeper, Alfred W. Pollard. And to him I told my simple tale, and asked his assistance. Mr. Pollard is himself a bibliographer of note in his special field, and my story was not without interest to him, but he refused to share my belief that the missing broadside was what I supposed it to be, laying much stress upon the black-letter feature as proof of its English origin. The unsuccessful search for the missing broadside had evidently been called to his notice, and the failure to produce anything in the millions of books catalogued in that vast collection, he considered a challenge to the efficiency of himself and his staff of assistants. A few days later, he acknowledged failure; but gave me the interesting information that in tracing the broadside back to its accession he had found that it was acquired by the Museum in the year 1865, and formed part of a bundle of miscellaneous matter, being considered of so little importance as not even to have been mentioned in the contents of the bundle. Printing of the letter F of the Catalogue was completed in 1888, and since that time an expansion of the classification of books upon the shelves had been made, from which dated its disappearance. He would not, however, discontinue his efforts to find it. After apologizing for giving him a "bad half-hour," which only the importance of the broadside excused, our second interview ended. On my last day in London, I went again with Mr. Stevens to call on Mr. Pollard about the matter, and told him that I had made my arrangements to fly from London to Paris on the morrow, and asked him if these old eyes of mine were never to behold the holy grail. "In black-letter?" he queried, touching the weak spot in my armor. "In duodecimo!" I countered, pointing to the rent in his own. And the third interview ended with his assurance that the search would go on until the missing broadside was found.

And there the matter rests, very much in the condition of the story of the cook who asked the skipper: "Is any thing lost· when you know where it is?" And to the skipper's gruff response, "Of course not," he pleasantly replied: "I am glad to know that our only iron soup kettle wasn't lost when it fell overboard into the Bay."

Through the courtesy of our fellow-members, Henry Edwards Huntington, Esquire, and the accomplished bibliographer and librarian of his unrivaled collection of books and art, George Watson Cole, the Society is permitted to give a reproduction from the only known copy of "The Book of General Lawes and Libertyes concerning the Inhabitants of the Massachusetts"— the long - lost Code of 1648. No copy or fragment of a copy was known to be extant for over two hundred and fifty years, when, in 1906, this copy was discovered in a small private library in England, and was sold to the late Edmund Dwight Church for the highest price ever paid for an American printed book— a record which is not likely to be surpassed. The almost miraculous recovery of this volume, will, I have given my reasons to hope, sometime have a counterpart in the recovery of the only known copy of the first work printed in the United States of America—The Oath of a Free man. From the year 1641, this bore the abbreviated title of the

FREEMANS OATH

I (A. B.) being by Gods providence an Inhabitant within the Jurisdiction of this Common-wealth, and now to be made free; doe heer freely acknowledge my self to be subject to the Government therof: and therfore do heer swear by the great and dreadfull Name of the Ever-living God, that I will be true and faithfull to the same, & will accordingly yeild assistance & support therunto, with my person and estate, as in equitie I am bound, and will also truly indeavour to maintein & preserve all the Liberties and Priviledges therof, submitting my self unto the wholsom Laws made and established by the same. And farther, that I will not plot or practice any evil against it, or consent to any that shall so doe; but will timely discover & reveal the same to lawfull authoritie now heer established, for the speedy prevention therof.

Moreover, I do solemnly binde my self in the sight of God, that when I shall be called to give my voice touching any such matter of this State, wherin Free-men are to deal; I will give my vote and *suffrage* as I shall in mine own conscience judge best to conduce and tend to the publick weal of the Body, without respect of persons, or favour of any man. So help me God in our Lord Jesus Christ. [1641.] From Code of 1648.

FREEMANS OATH

I [A. B.] being by Gods providence an inhabitant within the
Jurisdiction of this Common-wealth, and now to be made free;
doe here freely acknowledg my self to be subject to theGovern-
ment thereof: And therefore do here Swear by the great and
dreadfull Name of the Ever-living God, that I will be true and
faithfull to the same, and will accordingly yeild assistance and
support thereunto, with my person and estate, as in equity I
am bound, and will also truely indeavour to maintain and preserve all the Liberties and Priviledges thereof, submitting
my self unto the'wholsom Laws made and established by the
same. And farther, that I will not plot or practice an evill
against it, or consent to any that shall so doe; but will timely
discover and reveal the same to lawfull Authority now here
established, for the speedy prevention thereof.

Moreover, I do solemnly bind my self in the sight of God,
that when I shall be called to give my voice touching any such
matter of this State, wherein Free-men are to deal; I will give
my vote and suffrage as I shall in mine own conscience judg
best to conduce and tend to the publick weal of the Body,
without respect of persons, or favour of any man. So help
me God &c. [1641.] From Code of 1660.

It is Ordered and by this Court declared, that no man shall
be urged to take any Oath or subscribe to any *Articles,
Covenants* or *Remonstrances*, of publick and Civil nature, but
such as the Generall Court hath Considered, allowed and
required, and no Oath of any Magistrate or of any Officer, shall
bind him any further or longer, then he is Resident or Reputed
an Inhabitant of this Jurisdiction. [1641.]

Every Court in this Jurisdiction, where two Magistrates are
present, may admitt any church members that are fitt, to be
Freemen, giving them the Oath, and the Clerke of each Court,
shall certify their names to the Secretary at the next General
Court. [1641 [2]].

In 1643, the Colonies of Massachusetts-Bay, New
Plymouth, Connecticut, and New Haven, concluded a
Confederacy by which they entered into a solemn
compact to afford each other mutual advice and assistance on all necessary occasions, whether offensive,
defensive, or prudential. Among the reasons assigned
for this Union were the dependent condition of the
colonists; the vicinity of the French and Dutch, who
were inclined to make encroachments; the warlike

attitude of the neighboring Indians; the commence-
ment of civil war in England, and impracticability of
aid from thence in any emergency; and the sacred ties
of religion which already bound them. The Province
of Maine was not included because it was subject to
rulers of Episcopal tenets, and was infrequently an
asylum for excommunicants. This Union lasted for
forty years without any general Oath of Allegiance
being required from the inhabitants of the several
Colonies.

OATH OF FIDELITIE

I (A B) being by Gods providence an Inhabitant within the
Jurisdiction of this Common-wealth, doe freely and sincerely
acknowledge my selfe to be subject to the Government thereof.
And doe heer swear by the great and dreadful name of the Ever-
living God, that I will be true and faithfull to the same, and will
accordingly yeild assistance therunto, with my person and
estate, as in equitie I am bound: and will also truly indeavour
to maintein and preseve all the Liberties & Priviledges thereof,
submitting my self unto the wholsom Laws made, & established
by the same. And farther, that I will not plot or practice any
evil against it, or consent to any that shall so doe: but will timely
discover and reveal the same to lawfull Authoritie now heer
established, for the speedy preventing thereof. So help me
God in our Lord Jesus Christ. [1646.] From Code of 1648.

OATH OF FIDELITIE

I [A. B.] being by Gods providence an inhabitant within the
Jurisdiction of the Commonwealth, do freely and sincerely
acknowledge my selfe to be subject to the Government thereof.
And do here Swear by the great and dreadful name of the ever-
living God, that I will be true & faithfull to the same, and will
accordingly yeild assistance thereunto, with my person and
estate, as in equity I am bound: And will also truely endeavour
to Maintain and preserve all the Liberties & Priviledges thereof
submitting my self unto the wholesom Laws made, and established by the same.
And farther that I will not plot or practice any evill against
it, or consent to any that shall so do: but will timely discover
and reveal the same to lawfull Authority now here established,
for the speedy preventing thereof. So help me God in our Lord
Jesus Christ. [1646.] From Code of 1660.

To the end the body of the freemen may be preserved of honest and good men, It is Ordered, That henceforth no man shall be admitted to the freedome of this Common-wealth, but such as are members of some of the Churches, within the limits of this Iurisdiction; *And whereas many members of Churches to exempt themselves from Publick Service, will not come in to be made free-men,* It is Ordered, That no members of Churches within this Iurisidiction, shall be exempt from any publick service, they shall be chosen to, by the Inhabitants of the severall Townes, as Constables, Iurors, Select men, surveiors of the High-wayes. And if any such person shall refuse to serve in, or to take upon him any such Office, being legally chosen therunto, he shall pay for every such refusall, such fine, as the Town shall impose not exceeding *Twenty shillings* for one Offence. [1647.]

Any non freemen, who have taken or shall take the Oath of fidelity to this government could be jury men and vote in certain matters, after he had attained the age of 24 years. [1647.]

For as much as divers Inhabitants of this Jurisdiction who have long continued amongst us, receiving Protection, from this Government, have as we are informed uttered Offencive speeches, whereby their fidelity to this Government may justly be suspected, and also that divers strangers of forreign parts do repaire to us of whose fidelity we have not that Assurance which is Commonly required of all Governments.

It is therefore Ordered by this Court and the Authority thereof. That the County Courts or any one Magistrate out of Court, shall have power and is hereby Authorized to Require the Oath of fidelity of all settled Inhabitants amongst us who have not already taken the same, as also to Require the Oath under written, of all strangers, who after two months have their abode here; And if any Person shall refuse to take the Respective Oath, he or they shall be bound over to the next County Court or Court of Assistants, where if he shall refuse, he shall forfeit *five pound a week* for every week he shall Continue in this Jurisdiction after his sayd Refusall, unles he can give sufficient security to the satisfaction of the Court or Magistrate for his fidelity, during his or their residence amongst us.

STRANGERS OATH

You A. B. Do acknowledge your self subject to the Lawes of this Jurisdiction during your Residence under this Government, and do here Swear, by the Great Name of the Everliving GOD, and engage your self to be true and faithfull to the same, and not to plot, contrive, or conceal any thing that is to the hurt or detriment thereof. [1652.].

This was, apparently, aimed at the Quakers, whose offensive attitude towards the Government was made the subject of further drastic laws and orders by the General Court, in October, 1656, and May, 1658.

This Court having considered of the proposals presented to this Court by several of the inhabitants of the County of Middlesex; Do Declare and Order, That no man whosoever, shall be admitted to the Freedome of this Body Politick, but such as are members of some Church of Christ and in full Communion, which they declare to be the true intent of the ancient Law, *page the eighth of the second Book,* Anno. 1631. [1660.]

This was construed as being directed against the members of the Church of England, and was largely responsible for the strained relations with his Majesty's Commission in 1665. It was repealed before the 1672 Revision of the Laws.

For causes already mentioned the publication of the first Code of Laws, in 1648, was unnoticed in England; but it was very different with the publication of the second Code, in 1660. When it appeared its provisions were subjected to critical scrutiny by enemies of the Puritan Commonwealth, and the worst possible constructions placed upon them. In particular, the loyalty of the framers, who took an Oath of Fidelity to their Government, and none to the King, was questioned; and the provisions for the admission of freemen which, practically, prohibited members of the Church of England. By letter, his Majesty ordered a redress of these grievances, and appointed a Commission who proceeded, in a partisan manner, to execute their powers. In 1665, the Commissioners presented to the General Court a list of twenty-six changes which they desired to have made in the Code of 1660. The principal ones were the substitution of an acknowledgment of the royal authority for all expressions of the supremacy of the Commonwealth; a recognition of the Church of England; and a repeal of the long-standing limitation of citizenship to church members. To one or two of their points the General Court gave consent. A comparison with the Code of 1672, shows that while the recognition of his majesty's supremacy was allowed, in a score of instances the powers of the government under their Charter were asserted. The right of strangers to become citizens was nominally conceded, but on conditions which afforded only a minimum of relief to members of the Church of England.

On the 3 August, 1664 it was Ordered by the General Court:

In Answer to that part of his Majestyes Letter, of June 28, 1662, *concerning admission of freemen.* This Court doth Declare, That the Law prohibiting all persons, except Members of Churches, and, that also for allowance of them in any County Court, are hereby Repealed, And do hereby also Order and Enact That, from henceforth all English men presenting a Certificate under the hand of the Ministers, or Minister of the Place where they dwell, that they are Orthodox in Religion, and not vicious in their Lives, and also a certificate under the hands of the Select men of the place, or of the major Part of them, that they are Free-holders: and are for their own propper Estate (without heads of Persons) Rateable to the Country in a single Country Rate, after the usuall manner of valuation in the place where they live, to the full vallue of *Ten Shillings,* or that they are in full Communion with some Church amongst us; It shall be in the Liberty of all and every such Person or Persons, being *twenty-four* yeares of age, Householders and settled Inhabitants in this Jurisdiction, from time to time to themselves and their desires to this Court, for their addmittance to the freedome of this commonwealth, and shall be allowed the priviledge, to have such their desire Propounded and put to Vote in the General Court, for acceptance to the freedome of the body pollitick, by the sufferage of the major parte according to the Rules of our Patent. [1664.].

It was also Ordered by the General Court on the 19 October, 1664.

Forasmuch as several Persons who from time to time are to be made freemen, live remote and are not able without great trouble and charge to appear before this Court to take their respective Oaths: It is therefore Ordered, that henceforth it shall be in the power of any County Court, to administer the Oath of Freedome to any persons approved of by the General Court who shall desire the same, any Law or Custome to the contrary notwithstanding. [1664.]

And, at the May, 1665, session, to conform to the criticism of his Majesty's Commission concerning the Oath of Allegiance:

It is ordered by this Court, & the authority thereof, that the following oath be annexed vnto the oathes of euery freeman & oath of fidellity, & to the Gouerno͏ʳ, Dept͏⁻Gouerno͏ʳ, & Assistants, & to all other publicke officers, as followeth:—
The oath of a freeman & fidelity to runne thus:—

OATH OF FIDELITIE

Whereas I [A. B.] am an inhabitant within this Jurisdiction, Considering how I stand Obliged to the Kings Majesty, his heires and Successors by our Charter and the Government established thereby; Do Swear accordingly by the great and dreadfull Name of the Ever-Living God, that I will bear Faith and true Allegiance to our Soveraingn Lord the King, his Heires and Successors; and that I will be True and Faithfull to this Government, and accordingly yeild Assistance there-unto, with my person and estate, as in equity I am bound;

And will also truely endeavour to Maintain and Preserve all the Liberties and Priviledges thereof, Submiting my self unto the wholesom Laws made and established by the same.

And farther that I will not Plot or practice any evill against it, or consent to any that shall so do: but will timely discover and reveal the same to Lawfull Authority now here established, for the speedy preventing thereof. So help me God in our Lord Jesus Christ. [1665.]

FREEMANS OATH

Whereas I [A. B.] being an inhabitant of the Jurisdiction of the *Massachusets*, and now to be made free. Do hereby acknowledge my selfe to be subject to the Government thereof (Considering how I stand obliged to the Kings Majesty, his Heires and Successors, by our Charter and the Government established thereby Do Swear accordingly, by the Great and Dreadfull Name of the Ever-Living GOD, that I will bear Faith and true Alegiance to our Soveraigne Lord the King, his heires and Successors,) and that I will be true and Faithfull to the same, and will accordingly yeild Assistance and Support thereunto with my person and estate, as in equity I am bound; And will also truely endeavour to maintain and preserve all the Liberties and priviledges thereof, submitting my selfe to the wolesome Laws made and established by the same.

And farther that I will not Plot nor Practice any Evill against it, or consent to any that shall so do, but will timely discover and reveal the same to Lawfull Authority now here established, for the speedy prevention thereof.

Moreover I do Solemnly bind my selfe in the sight of God, that when I shall be called to give my Voyce touching any such matter of this State wherein Freemen are to deal, I will give my Vote and Suffrage as I shall in mine own Conscience judge best to conduce and tend to the Publick Weale of the body, without respect of persons or favour of any man. So help me God in our Lord Jesus Christ. [1665.]

The oath of the Goūno', Dept Goūno', & other publicke officers, to runne thus:—
Whereas I, A. B., am chosen Gouerno', &c., considering how I stand obliged to the kings majesty, his heires & successors, by our charter and the gouerment here established thereby, doe sweare, &c, as aboue. [1665.]

In their demand for changes in the 1660 Book of the General Laws and Liberties, the Commissioners in their 14th section proposed: "That, page 33, 'none be admitted freemen but such as are members of some of the churches wᵗʰ in the limitts of this jurisdiction' may be explained, & comphend such as are members of yᵉ church of England."

At the General Court of 23 May, 1666:
It is ordered that the Secretary, at the request of all such as are admitted to the freedome of this Colony or any in their behalf, give a true copy out of this Courts Records, of their names, by them to be delivered to the clerks or recorders of those Courts in the severall Counties to which they do belong, with a copy of the Oath of Freemen as it is now stated, that they may there take their Oathes &c. [1666.]

At the General Court of 15 October, 1673:
As an addition to the Law, title Freemen, section the third, it is ordered by this Court and the authority thereof that henceforth the names of such as desire to be admitted to the freedome of this Comon-wealth, not being members of churches in full comunion, shall be entred wᵗʰ the secretary, from tjme to tjme, at the Court of election, and read ouer before the whole Court sometime that sessions and shall not be put to vote in the Court till the Court of election next followg. [1673.]
This order of Court was repealed 9 February 1682/3.

Att a Generall Court, held at Boston, 10ᵗʰ of October, 1677.
Whereas many secret attempts haue binn lately made by euil minded persons to set fire in the toune of Boston and other places, tending to the destruction of the whole, this Court doeth account it their duty to vse all lawfull meanes to discouer such persons and prevent the like for time to come.

Bee it therefore ordered & enacted by this Court and the Authority thereof, That the Law, *title* Oathes and Subscriptions, page 120 sect. 2., requiring all persons, as well inhabitants as strangers, (that have not taken it) to take the Oath of Fidelity to the Country, be revived and put in practice through this Jurisdiction. And for the more effectual execution thereof, It is ordered by this Court; That the select men, Constables, and Tithing-men, in every town do, once every quarter of a year so proportion and divide the precincts of each town, and go from house to house, and take an exact list of the Names, quality and callings of every person, whether Inhabitant or Stranger, that have not taken the said Oath, and cannot make due proof thereof; and the Officers aforesaid are hereby required forthwith to return the names of such persons unto the next magistrate, or County Court, or chief military officer in the town where no Magistrate is, who are required to give such persons the said Oath prescribed in the Law, wherein not only Fidelity to the Country, but Allegiance to our King, is required; And all such as take the said oath shall be Recorded and Enrolled in the County Records by the clerk of each County Court. And all such as refuse to take the said Oath, they shall be proceeded against as the said Law directs. And further, this Court doth Declare; That all such refusers to take the said Oath shall not have the benefit of our Laws to Implead, Sue, or recover any Debt in any Court or Courts within this Jurisdiction, nor have protection from this Government whilest they continue in such obstinate refusal.

And furthermore, It is Ordered; That if any Officer intrusted with the Execution of this Order, do, neglect, or omit his or their duty therein, they shall be fined according to their demerits, not exceeding five pounds for one offence, being complained of, or presented to the County Courts or Court of Assistants, And this Law to be forthwith Printed and Published, and effectually executed from and after the last of *November* next. And that all persons that administer the Oath abovesaid, shall in like manner make return of the Names of such persons so sworn to the respective Clerks of the County Courts. Made October 10, 1677.

Att the second sessions of the Gen ll Court held at Boston, 2 October, 1678.

Whereas it hath pleased his most excellent Majesty, our gracious king by his letter bearing date the twenty-seventh of Aprill, 1678, to signifie his Royall pleasure, That the Authority of this his Colony of Massachusetts in New-England, do give forth Orders that the Oath of Allegiance, as it is by Law established within his Kingdome of England, be administred and taken by all his subjects within this Colony who are of years to take an oath:

In Obedience whereunto, and as a demonstration of our Loyalty; It is ordered and enacted by this Court and the Authority thereof, that, as the members of this Court now sitting have readily taken the Oath of Allegiance, so, by their Example and Authority, they do require and command that the same Oath be given and taken by all his Majesties subjects within this Jurisdiction that are of sixteen years of age and upwards. And to the end this Order be duely executed, it is hereby Ordered, that a convenient number of printed Copies of the said Oath of Allegiance, exactly agreeing with the written copy inclosed in his majesties Letter, and signed by the Secretary of State, to be sent forth unto every Magistrate and Justice of peace, and to the Constable of every town within this Jurisdiction.

And it is further Ordered that the Magistrates and Justices, or such as are Commissioned with Magistratical Authority in every County of this Colony do with all convenient speed repair to the several Towns and Villages within this Jurisdiction, at such time, and in such order as they best may, and accomplish the same; giving forth their warrant to the Constables of each Town to convene all the inhabitants of the Age abovesaid, and taking their names in writing, administer the said Oath of Allegiance to each of them, and return their Names to the Recorder of each County Court to be enrolled. And if any shall refuse to take the said Oath, or absent themselves unless in case of sickness, the Names of such shall be returned to the Recorder of the County, who are to be proceeded against by the County Courts respectively, for the first offence whereof he is legally convicted, to pay such a fine as the County Court shall impose, not exceeding five pounds, or three Moneths Imprisonment in the common prison or house of Correction: And for the second offence whereof he shall be lawfully convicted, what summe the County Court shall inflict, provided it exceed not ten pounds, or six Moneths Imprisonment without Baile, or Mainprise. [1678.]

The officials of the Government, ignoring the copy of the Oath of Allegiance given them by the royal commissioners, took the Oath in Court as it is given in Michael Dalton's "The Countrey Justice,"—a work of much esteem in its time, which passed through some ten or eleven editions, three of which are in the valuable Library of this Society, and one of them, there is reason to believe, may have been the volume used in this historical incident,—all of them declaring that the same is to be understood as not infringing the liberties and privileges granted in his Majesty's royal Charter to this Colony of the Massachusetts.

Regarding the manner of taking the Oath; the New England custom was by holding up the right hand, as opposed to the custom in England of holding, or laying the hand on the Bible, or kissing it. This was one of the irritating questions in dispute between the Colonists and the Andros faction. Samuel Sewall, in his Diary, under date of June 11, 1686, says: "I read the Oath myself holding the book in my left hand, and holding up my right hand to Heaven." And, in 1687, Increase Mather discoursed on the "laying the hand on and kissing the booke in swearing." This question continued to irritate, and was one of the predisposing causes of the Revolutionary War in the Province of New York. In 1772, a Bill was lost in Council, "For Removing Doubts in the administration of Oaths." This Bill was designed to favor a number of people, chiefly from Scotland and the north of Ireland, who held conscientious scruples against the present legal form of kissing the Bible; and allow them to use the form in use in Scotland and the New England Colonies of lifting up the right hand. The weight of Episcopal authority denied them this right.

In the colonization of New England the figure of John Winthrop looms colossal. Given time, he would have built an Empire whose only ruler would have been the Lord of Hosts. He can hardly be called a Puritan—his conversion came too late—but he was a Congregationalist. His method was so simple as to be open to the understanding of anyone, but it was a firm principle of government. As an illustration: when he was appealed to by a small group of settlers near the border line of New Hampshire for information as to how they could become freemen of the Colony of

Massachusetts-Bay, his reply was: "Get a Minister."
When they answered that they had no Minister, and
did not know where to get one, again came back his
uncompromising reply: "Get a Minister." In this
reply rested his whole system of colonization. It was
simplicity itself. The English Government recog-
nized its power when, by Proclamation, they endeavored to prevent the emigration of Puritan
Ministers from England. "Get a Minister!" Gather
about him! Build him a church, and homes for your-
selves and families. This done, you have a Plantation. When you have thus qualified to become freemen, and have taken the Oath of a Freeman, you will
be entitled to hold office; assist in framing laws, and
enforcing those already made; and, as members of the
Commonwealth, be assured that all your rights will be
protected. This principle of government was firm,
but not repellent. If you could not conform to it there
was no reason for remaining among them. The world
was wide enough for every one. And you could go to
Maine, or Rhode Island. Under it was formed a
government that has never been equalled in prosperity,
morality and all that makes for happiness. No less a
personage than Hugh Peters has declared that in the
six years of his residence in the Colony of Massachusetts-Bay, he had never seen a drunken man or heard
a profane oath.

The limits of their territory they continually en-
larged by firmly insisting upon the border lines of
their Patent, and even stretching them when near
some natural boundary; by purchasing the rights of
New Plymouth in the Colony of Maine, for 400
pounds, they added a tract of seven hundred square
miles; by the purchase of the Gorges Patent, for 1,250
pounds sterling, they acquired a jurisdiction over the
rest of the Province of Maine which made it a District
of Massachusetts down to the year 1820. There has
been a good deal of sympathy, and many unnecessary
tears have been shed over the so-called banishment of

Roger Williams to Rhode Island; but it was his friend, John Winthrop, who whispered in his ear the desirability of the location of the Providence Plantations. And there was no reason why Roger Williams could not have gone out from Salem with head erect, and with his gaze fixed on the stars, as every good missionary should go, knowing that the powers of the government of Massachusetts-Bay was as much behind his settlement, without an Oath, as it was behind the colonists of Connecticut, and New Haven, who had gone out from Cambridge, Watertown and Roxbury, carrying with them the Oath of a Freeman as a principle of their governments. In the Union of the Colonies of Massachusetts-Bay, New Plymouth, Connecticut, and New Haven, of which John Winthrop was the first President, a new idea was advanced in his system of government, which eventually attained greater results.

It cannot be said that John Winthrop accomplished these things unaided. There were others who ably assisted him, whose names, also, should be held in honored remembrance. But through it all, can be seen the firm, directing mind and purpose of a man whose vision looked beyond his present to a future, and a Republic that was to be.

And this is why our people should look upon The Oath of a Freeman, which was his work, not alone as the glorious first fruit of the Printing-Press in this Country; but also as a great state paper which accomplished without bloodshed, on a smaller scale it is true, all that was achieved, one hundred and thirty-seven years later, after seven years of warfare, through the Declaration of Independence.

In Connecticut and New Haven Colonies.

The colonists of Connecticut, in the main, followed closely the general system of laws of the Massachusetts Bay Colony, from which they had emigrated. Their

form of government was theocratic, the Oath of a
Freeman being the test of citizenship. The settlers of
Windsor, who came from Dorchester with John War-
ham, in 1635, did not, however, make church member-
ship a necessary qualification for holding civil office.
The settlers of Guilford, who were joined to New
Haven Colony, exercised their powers of government
by a system which conformed to the grant from Lord
Say and Brook to Theophilus Eaton and his company.
Like that at New Haven it was an aristocracy, but
modelled in a singular way. As a part of New Haven
Colony they were entitled to one Magistrate, who was
their head and invested with the whole executive and
judicial power. The settlers were divided into two
classes, freemen and planters. The freemen could
consist only of those who were church members, and
partook of the sacrament. They were all under oath
agreeably to their form of government. Out of their
number were chosen three or four deputies to sit with
the Magistrate in General Courts, and all public
officers. The planters consisted of all inhabitants
above the age of twenty-one years, with a certain
estate, which qualified them to vote in town meetings.

5 to Apr 1638.   A gen'all Cort at Hartford.

Forasmuch as it has pleased the Allmighty God by the wise
disposition of his diuyne pruidence so to Order and dispose of
things that we the Inhabitants and Residents of Windsor,
Hartford and Wethersfield are now cohabiting and dwelling in
and vppon the River of Conectecotte and the Lands thereunto
adioyneing; And well knowing where a people are gathered
togather the word of God requires that to mayntayne the
peace and vnion of such a people there should be an orderly and
decent Gouerment established according to God, to order and
dispose of the affayres of the people at all seasons as occation
shall require: doe therefore assotiate and conioyne our selues
to be as one publike State or Comonwelth; and doe, for our
selues and our Successors and such as shall be adioyned to vs
att any tyme hereafter, enter into Combination and Confederation togather, to mayntayne and prsearue the liberty and
purity of the gospell of our Lord Jesus wch we now prfesse, as
also the disciplyne of the Churches wch according to the truth

of the said gospell is now practiced amongst vs; As also in o^r Ciuill Affaires to be guided and gouerned according to such Lawes, Rules, Orders and decrees as shall be made, ordered & decreed, as followeth: [The eleven Fundamentalls.] [1638.]

In Connecticut, it would appear that the Oath of Fidelity required of all that were admitted freemen up to July 1640, was as follows:

An Oath for Paqua¹ and the Plantations there:

I A. B. being by the P^ruidence of God an inhabitant wthin the Jurisdiction of Conectecotte, doe acknowledge my selfe to be subject to the gou^rment thereof, and doe sweare by the great and dreadfull name of the eu^r liueing God to be true and faythfull vnto the same, and doe submitt boath my P^rson & estate thereunto, according to all the holsome lawes & orders that ether are or hereafter shall be there made by lawfull authority: And that I will nether plott nor practice any euell agaynst the same, nor consent to any that shall so doe, but will tymely discou^r the same to lawfull authority established there; and that I will maynetayne, as in duty I am bownd, the honor of the same & of the lawfull Magestrats thereof, promoteing the publike good thereof, whilst I shall so continue an Inhabitant there, and whensou^r I shall give my vote, suffrage or p^rxy, being cauled thereunto touching any matter wch conserns this Comonwelth, I will giue y^t as in my conscience may conduce to the best good of the same, wthout respect of p^rson or favor of any man; So helpe me God in the Lo: Jesus Christ. [1640.]

The Oath of a Freeman

I, A. B. being by the P^ruidence of God an Inhabitant wthin the Jurisdiction of Conectecotte, doe acknowledge myselfe to be subiecte to the Gouerment thereof, and doe sweare by the great and fearefull name of the euerliueing God, to be true and faythfull vnto the same, and doe submitt boath my p^rson and estate thereunto, according to all the holsome lawes and orders that there are, or here after shall be there made, and established by lawfull authority, and that I will nether plott nor practice any euell ag^t the same, nor consent to any that shall so doe, but will tymely discouer the same to lawfull authority there established; and that I will, as I am in duty bownd, mayntayne the honner of the same and of the lawfull Magestratts thereof, p^rmoting the publike good of y^t, whilst I shall soe continue an inhabitant there; and whensoeu^r I shall giue my voate or suffrage touching any matter wch conserns this Comon welth being cauled there unto, will give y^t as in my conscience I shall judge may conduce to the best good of the same, wthout respect of p^{r}sons or favor of any man. Soe helpe me God in o^r Lord Jesus Christe. Aprill the xth, 1640.

At a Generall Assembly held at Hartford, April 20th, 1665, there was presented to the Court the Propositions of his Majesty's Royal Commission which were read and answered as follows;

1. That all householders inhabiting this Colony take the oath of allegiance, and that the administration of justice be in his Majesties name.

To this we returne, that according to his Majesties pleasure exprest in o^r Charter, o^r Gouernour formerly hath nominated and appoynted meet persons to administer the oath of allegiance, whoe haue, according to their order, administred the s^d oath to seuerall persons allready; and the administration of justice amongst us hath been, is and shall be in his Majesties name.

2nd Propos: That all men of competent estates and of ciuill conuersation, though of different judgments, may be admitted to be freemen, and haue liberty to chuse or to be chosen officers, both military and ciuill.

To the 2d, our order for admission of freemen is consonant wth that proposition.

3. Propos: That all persons of ciuill liues may freely injoy the liberty of their consciences, and the worship of God in that way which they thinke best, prouided that this liberty tend not to the disturbance of the publique, nor to the hindrance of the mayntenance of Ministers regularly chosen in each respectiue parish or township.

To the 3d Propos: We say, we know not if any one that hath bin troubled by us for attending his conscience, prouided he hath not distu^{r}bed the publique.

4 Propos: That all lawes and expressions in lawes, derogatory to his Majestie, if any such haue bin made in these late troublesome times, may be repealed, altered and taken off the file.

To the 4th p^{r}pos: We return, we know not of any lawe or expressions in any law that is derogatory to his Majesty amongst us; but if any such be found, we count it o^r duty to repeal, alter it, and take it off the file, and this we attended upon the receipt of our Charter. [1665].

At a Gen^{ll} Assembly for election held at Hartford, May 11, '65. This Court declare that it is their full sense and determination that such persons as are or hereafter shalbe approued to be freemen of this Corporation shal take yᵉ Oath that is already established vpon record to be administered to yᵉ respectiue freemen: And further, that all such as shal refuse to take the said oath, though otherwise approued p'sons yet shal not p'take of the privilidges of those that have bene formally incorporated into this civil society, vntil yᵉ said Oath be administred vnto them: Provided that this order includes not either freemen formerly admitted and sworne or Assistants and Comissioners that haue taken their corporal oaths or Deputies that haue bene accepted into yᵉ Genˡˡ Assembly to assist in ye concernments of this corporation. [1665.]

In New Haven Colony.

"On the 4ᵗʰ day of the 4ᵗʰ month called June 1639, all the free planters of the town to be called a year later Newhaven, assembled together in a general meetinge to consult about settling ciuill Gouernmᵗ according to God. * * * Mr. John Davenport propounded divers (6) quæries to them publiquely praying them to consider seriously * * * and to giue their answers in such sort as they would be willing they should stand upon recorde for posterity."

These six fundamental agreements were assented to by the lifting up of hands twice: once at the proposal and again after when the written words were read unto them.

And on the 25th of October next, the following charge was given and accepted by them:

Freeman's Charge

Yow shall neither plott, practise, nor consent, to any euill, or hurt, against this Jurisdiction, or any part of it, nor against The Civill Gouerment here established: And if you shall know any person or persons wᶜʰ intend, plott, or conspire anything, wᶜʰ tends to the hurt, or prjudice, of the same, you shall timely discouer the same to Lawfull Authority here established, and you shall assist, and be helpfull, in all the affaires of the Jurisdiction, and by all meanes shall promoue the publique wellfare of the same, according to yoʳ place, abillity, and opportunity; you shall giue due honoʳ to the Lawfull Magistrats, and shall be obedient, and subject, to all the wholesome Lawes, and Orders, allready made, or wᶜʰ shall be hereafter made, by

Lawfull Authority afforesaide, and that both in yo[r] person, and estate, and when you shall be duely called, to giue yo[r] vote, or suffrage, in any Election, or touching any other matter, w[ch] concerneth this Common wellth, yow shall giue it, as in yo[r] conscience, you shall judg may conduse to the best good of the same. [1639.]

At A Gen. Court held att Newhaven the 3[d] of Aprill 1644. This day, a forme of an oath for the Governo[r] and magistrats to take, and another forme of an oath to be imposed upon all the inhabitants w[t]hin this jurisdiction was propounded to the consideratiō of the court, who, after some serious debate and consideratiō rested satisfyed w[t]h the said formes. And there-vpon ordered thatt itt should be forthw[t]h putt in executiō, and whereas the Governo[r] doth shortly intend a journey to Stamforde on other occasions, the Court desired him to im-prove thatt opportunity, both at Stamforde and att Milford, for the giveing of the oath, and the like att Guilforde in time convenient. Itt was further ordered thatt no person or persons shall hereafter be admitted as an inhabitant in this jurisdictiō or any of the plantations therein butt he or they shall take the said oath vpon his or their admittance.

On the 23 of June, 1644, The formes of two oathes were pro-pounded to the Court to be taken the next second day in the morning, by all the inhabitants in this plantatiō, one of them is to be taken by all, and the other by the Governo[r] onely.

Att a Gen[rll] Court held att Newhaven the 1[t] of July, 1644. The Governo[r] tooke this oath as followeth,

I [Theophilus Eaton] being att a Gen[rll] Co[rt] in October last, chosen Governo[r] w[t]hin Newhaven Jurisdictiō for a yeare then to ensue, and vntill a new Governo[r] be chosen, do sweare by the great and dreadfull name of the ever living God, to promove the publique good and peace of the same, according to the best of my skill, and will allso maintaine all the lawfull priviledges of this comōwealth, according to the fundamentall order and agreem[t] made for governm[t] in this jurisdictiō, and in like manner will endeuo[r] thatt all wholsome lawes thatt are or shall be made by lawfull authority here established be duely executed, and will further the executiō of justice according to the righteous rules of Gods worde, so help me God in o[r] Lord Jesus Christ.

The Governo[r] haveing allso received the

OATH OF FIDELITY

as followeth,

I [Theophilus Eaton] being by the providence of God an inhabitant w[t]hin Newhaven Jurisdictiō, doe acknowledge myselfe to be subject to the goverm^t thereof, and doe sweare by the great and dreadfull name of the ever living God, to be true and faithfull vnto the same, and doe submitt both my person and my whole estate thervnto according to all the wholsome lawes and orders thatt for present are or hereafter shall be there made and established by lawfull authority, and thatt I will neither plott nor practise any evill agst the same, nor consent to any thatt shall so doe, butt will timely discover the same to lawfull authority here established, and thatt I will as I am in duety bounde, maintaine the hono^r of the same and off the lawfull magistrates thereoff, promoting the publique good of the same whilest I shall continue an inhabitant there. And whensoever I shall be duely called a free burgesse, according to the fundamentall order and agreem^t for governm^t in this jurisdictiō to give my vote or suffrage touching any matter wch concerneth this comō wealth, I will give itt as in my conscience I shall judge may conduce to the best good of the same w^thout respect of persons, So help me God in our Lord Jesus Christ.

Then he gave itt to all those whose names are herevnder written, [Two hundred and sixteen names.] [1644.]

In May, 1665, the Colonies of Connecticut, and New Haven were united as the Colony of Connecticut in New England.

Oath of Allegiance

Administered at New Haven, in May 1666, under powers granted by Governor John Winthrop, according to his Maj^{ties} Charter granted to this Colony of Connecticut in New England.

You J[asper] C[rane], doe sweare faith and Allegeance to his Maj^{tie} Charles ye Second, as duty binds according to ye word of God. And yo^u doe hereby acknowledge that the Pope, nor any other potentate hath powe^r or autority or iurisdiction in any of his Maj^{ties} dominions, and y^t only his Matie our soverⁿ Lord King Charles hath under God, supreme power in his Maties dominions. And I doe abhor ye detestable opinion y^t the pope hath pow^r to Depose princes. And this I doe from my hart, soe help me God.

On the 31 October, 1687, Sir Edmund Andros, Knt. took over into his hands the government of the Colony of Connecticut in New England.

In Rhode Island and Providence Plantations.

The settlement of Rhode Island by Roger Williams, being partly occasioned by his refusal to take either the

Oath of Fidelity, or the Stranger's Oath to the Colony of Massachusetts-Bay will account for the absence of all Oaths of Allegiance in the early history of the Colony which he founded. From the first settlement of the Colony of Rhode Island and Providence Plantations to the present time an Oath could not be required of any one; but in its place is required a property qualification and an Affirmation.

Civil Compact

We whose names are hereunder, desirous to inhabit in the town of Providence, do promise to subject ourselves in active and passive obedience to all such orders or agreements as shall be made for public good of the body in an orderly way, by the major consent of present inhabitants, masters of families, incorporated together in a Towne fellowship, and others whom they shall admit unto them only in civil things. [Richard Scott, and twelve others.] August the 20th, [1637.]

This limiting of the powers of town meetings to "civil things," is the first expression in the new world of a severance of the bonds of Church and State, and of that principle of freedom of conscience for which the founder had contended. This first Civil Compact was followed, on the 7th day of the first month, 1638, by the settlers at Aquidneck, with a

Second Civil Compact

We whose names are underwritten do here, solemnly, in the presence of Jehovah incorporate ourselves into a Bodie Politick and as he shall help, will submit our persons, lives and estates unto our Lord Jesus Christ, the King of Kings and Lord of Lords and to all those perfect and most absolute lawes of his given us in his holy word of truth, to be guided and judged thereby. Exod. 24. 3. 4, 2 Cron. 11.3. 2 Kings, 11. 17. [William Coddington, and eighteen others.]

The 7th of the first month, 1638. We that are Freemen Incorporate of this Bodie Politick do Elect and Constitute William Coddington, Esquire, a Judge amongst us, and so covenant to yield all due honour unto him according to the lawes of God, and so far as in us lyes to maintaine the honour and privileges of his place which shall hereafter be ratifyed according unto God, the Lord helping us so to do.

William Aspinwall, Sec'ry.

I, William Coddington, Esquire, being called and chosen by the Freemen Incorporate of this Bodie Politick, to be a Judge amongst them, do covenant to do justice and Judgment impartially according to the lawes of God, and to maintaine the Fundamentall Rights and Privileges of this Bodie Politick, which shall hereafter be ratifyed according unto God, the Lord helping us so to do.

On the 3d Month, 13 day, 1638. It is ordered that none shall be received as inhabitants or Freemen to build or plant upon the Island but such as shall be received in by the consent of the Bodye, and do submitt to the government that is or shall be established, according to the word of God. [1638.]

From this arrangement, the first recorded Act regarding freemen in the Colony, a minority seceded, taking the Records with them, and drew up the following instrument:

It is agreed

By vs whose hands are underwritten, to propagate a Plantation in the midst of the Island or elsewhere; And doe engage ourselves to bear equall charges, answerable to our strength and estates in common; and that our determinations shall be by major voice of judge and elders; the Judge to have a double voice. [William Coddington, and eight others.] On the 28th of the 2d Month, 1639.

Agreeing and ordering that the Plantation now begun shall be called Newport.

The remaining members of the Aquidneck settlement then organized a new government.

Aprill the 30th, 1639.

We whose names are underwritten doe acknowledge ourselves the legall subjects of his Majestie King Charles, and in his name doe hereby binde ourselves into a civill body Politicke, assenting unto his lawes according to right and matters of justice. [William Hutchinson, and thirty associates.]

By the Body Politicke on the Ile of Agethnec, inhabiting this present, 25 of 9 = month, 1639.

In the fourteenth yeare of y^e Raign of our Sovereign Lord King Charles. It is agreed, That as natural subjects to our Prince, and subject to his Lawes, all matters that concerne the Peace shall be by those that are officers of the Peace transacted; And all actions of the Case or Dept, shall be in such

Courts as by order are here appointed, and by such Judges as are Deputed: Heard and Legally Determined.

At the Generall Court of Election began and held at Portsmouth, from the 16th of March to the 19th of the same mo., 1641.

1. It was ordered and agreed before the Election, that an Ingagement by oath should be taken of all the officers of this Body now to be elected, as likewise for the time to come; the ingagement which the severall officers of the State shall give is this; To the execution of this office I judge myself bound before God to walk faithfully, and this I profess in y⁰ presence of God.

3. It is ordered and unanimously agreed upon that the Government which this Bodie Politick doth attend vnto in this Island, and the Jurisdiction thereof, in favour of our Prince is a Democracie, or popular Government; that is to say, It is in the Powre of the Body of Freemen orderly assembled, or the major part of them, to make or constitute Just Lawes, by which they will be regulated, and to depute from among themselves such Ministers as shall see them faithfully executed between Man and Man.

16. It is ordered that Ingagement shall be taken by the Justices of the Peace in their Quarter Sessions of all men or youth above fifteen years of age, eyther by the oath of Fidelity, or some other strong cognizance.

28. It is ordered and received, that the Ingagement that already was given by the Freemen was and is of the same force as that oath is which is authorized to be administered to the Inhabitants, which oath Nicholas Easton, Rob't Jeoffreys, and Wm. Dyre did take in presence of the Courte.

29. It is ordered, that if any person or persons on the Island, whether Freeman or Inhabitant, shall by any meanes open or covert, endeavour to bring in any other Powre than what is now established (except it be from our Prince by lawfull commission), shall be accounted a delinquent under the head of Perjurie.

30. It is ordered, that the Law of the last Court made concerning Libertie of Conscience in point of Doctrine is perpetuated.

THE ENGAGEMENT OF THE OFFICERS

You, A. B. being called and chosen vnto public employment, and the office of——, by the free vote and consent y⁰ Inhabitants of the Province of Providence Plantations (now orderly met), do, in the present Assemblie, engage yourself faithfully and truly to the utmost of your power to execute the commission committed vnto you; and do hereby promise to do neither more nor less in that respect than that which the Colonie have or shall authorize you to do according to the best of your understanding.

THE RECIPROCAL ENGAGEMENT OF THE STATE TO Y^E OFFICERS

We, the Inhabitants of the Province of Providence Plantations being here orderly met, and having by free vote chosen you——, to public office and officers for the due administration of Justice and the execution thereof throughout the whole Colonie, do hereby engage ourselves to the utmost of our power to support and vphold you in your faithfull performance thereof. [1641.]

This Engagement was also agreed to by the Court of Commissioners and Election. September ye 13th, 1654.

It is ordered by the present Assemblie, that this is ye engagement of ye Generall officers any former forme to the contrarie notwithstandinge.

At the General Court of the 21st of May, 1661, the words: "in his Majesties name" was added after ("now orderly met").

And Att a Generall Assembly of the Collony of Rhode Iland and Providence Plantations the 4th of May, 1664:

This Assembly alsoe declareth against any parson acting in any publike office, except hee first take the engagement according to the forme hear subjoyned.

You, A. B., &c., sollemly engage to be true and faythfull vnto our Soveraigne Lord the King, Charles the Second, of England, Scotland, France and Ireland, and dominiones and terrytoryes therevnto belonging; and to his sayd Majesty, his heirs and successors, true allegeance to beare and exicute your commission, charge and office, according to the best of your skill and knowledge without partiallyty or affection to any; and that according to the lawes already established, or to be established in this Colony. This ingagement you make and ingage to obsearve, vnder the penalty of perjury. . . .

At the taking of the ingagement by any, ther must bee a re-engagement given in the Colloneys name, to stand by and assist such parsones in the exicution of ther offices and performance of ther dutyes.

It is alsoe the pleasuer and appoynment of this Generall Assembly, that none presume to vote in the matters afforesayd, but such whome this Generall Assembly expresly by ther writting shal admit as freemen.

The 19th of the iith Month, 1645. Wee whose names are heere after Subscribed, having obteyned a free Grante of

Twenty five Akers of Land a peece with right of Commoning, according to the said proportion of Land; from the free Jnhabitants of this Towne of providence; doe thankfully acsept of the same; And heereby doe promise to yield Actiue; or passiue Obeydience to the authority of　　　established in this Collonye; according to our Charter; and to all Such wholesome Lawes & Orders, that are or shall be made, by the major consent of this Towne of Providence; As alsoe not to clayme any Righte, to the Purchasse of the Said plantation; Nor any privilidge of Vote in Towne Affaires; untill we shall be received as free=Men of the said Towne of Providence. [1645.]

THE PREAMBLE TO THE LAW AGAINST PERJURY

Forasmuch as the consciences of sundry men, truly conscionable, may scruple the giving or the taking of an oath, and it would be nowise suitable to the nature and constitution of our place, who profess ourselves to be men of different consciences and not one willing to force another to debar such as cannot do so, either from bearing office among us or from giving in testimony in a case depending; be it enacted by the authority of this present Assembly, that a solemn profession or testimony in a court of record, or before a judge of record, shall be accounted, throughout the whole colony, of as full force as an oath. [1647.]

This is the more remarkable because at this time the Friends did not yet as a distinct Society, hold to the unlawfulness of oaths. And it is in complete concordance with the teachings of Roger Williams.

Acts and Orders of the Generall Assembly, sitting at Newport, May the 3, 1665.

Ordered, that this following shall be the forme for engaging all officers in this Collony, called to place of publicke concernment, &c., for the administration of justice, (viz):

Whereas, you are, A. B., by the free vote of the freemen of this Collony of Rhode Island and Providence Plantations, &c., called and chosen vnto the place and office of ——, in the said Collony, &c., doe sollemly engage true eleageance vnto his Majestye, his heires and successors, to beare, and in your said office equall justice and right to doe vnto all persones within this jurisdiction to the vtmost or best of your skill and ability without partiality, according to the laws established, or that shall be established in this said jurisdiction; [according to the Charter as well in matters military as civill.] And this engagement you make and give vpon the perill of the penalty of perjury.

The reciprocall engagement is as follows, ordered to be given by he that takes or administers the abovesaid engagement.

I doe, in the name and behalfe of this Collony, &c., re-ingage to stand by you and to support you by all due assistance and incouradgment in your performance and execution of your aforesaid office according to your engagement.

Ordered, that the forme of engagement aforesaid shall be used vntill further order; any former order or forme vsed or prescribed to the contrary, or differing herefrom notwithstanding. [1665.] These forms were re-enacted in 1677.

The Commission appointed by the King to assert the rights of the Crown to the seven New England Colonies, as the first of the propositions of his Majestys will and pleasure in Rhode Island, proposed:

That all householders inhabiting this Collony take the oath of alleagence and the administration of justice be in his Majestyes name.

Wherevpon, and in a deep sence of his Majestyes most Royall and wonderful grace and favour more pertickerlerly . . . in his letters pattents . . . in which is expresed his . . . indulgence extended to tender consiences, differing in matters of religious worshipe and conceanments; and more especially in matters of formes of oathes and cerimonyes or circumstances relating therevnto, . . . considering therein the liberty of concience therein granted.

The Assembly doe with one consent . . . in all cheerfull obediance . . . and therein minding the preveledge granted to tender conciences, doe in the first place order and declare: that whereas in this Collony it hath ben alwayes accounted and granted a liberty to such as make a scruple of swearing and taken an oath, that in stead thereof they shall engage, under the penalty of false swearing, though they sweare not in publicke engagement, as well as if they did sweare, that therefore this most loyall and resonable engagement be given by all men capable within this jurisdiction for their allegiance to the King, &c.

The forme of which engagement shall be as followeth:

You, A. B., sollemly and sincearly engage true and faithfull aleagiance vnto his Majestye Charles the Second, King of England, his heires and successors, to beare and due obediance vnto the lawes established, from time to time in this jurisdiction, to yeald vnto the vtmost of your power, according to the previlidge by his said Majesty granted, in religioues and civill concearnments to this Collony in the Charter; which said engagement you make vnder the perill and penalty of perjury. [1665.]

They further ordered that "this engagement shall be administered to all that are already admitted freemen, and that no man shall be admitted a freeman, and all men that are householders or aged eighteen or more, shall take the engagement or loose the priviledge of freemen until they give the engagement premised." The passage of this law led to a long agitation by those who thought it to be hard on the consciences by many whom it rendered incapable from carrying on the affairs of the corporation. And, in the following year, the Assembly ordered and declared, "That such as are free in their conscience so to do, give the Engagement, or if they rather choose to give the oath of allegiance now required in England, that shall be taken; but if there are some words in either which, in conscience they cannot condescend to say or use, may in open court, or before two Magistrates adopt in equivalent words significant of allegiance and submission to yield obedience actively and passively, to the laws made by virtue of his Majesty's authority, he shall be restored or admitted as freeman, any former law to the contrary notwithstanding."

At a Court held in his Majesty's name, and under his authority, at the towne of Westerly, in the King's Province, the 17th of September, 1679.

The inhabitants of Westerly, being by warrant required to appeare at this Court to give the oath of allegiance to his Majesty, and of fidellity to his Majesty's authority for this Collony, these persons hereunder named appeared and gave oath, viz. [Thirty-three names.]

The oath given by the above written persons was in these followinge words:

I doe truly and sincerely acknowledge, profess, testify and declare in my conscience before God and the world, that our Soverreign Lord, King Charles, is lawfull and rightfull King of the Realm of England, and of all other his dominions and countries; and that the Pope, neither of himselfe, nor by any authority of the Church, or See of Rome, or by any other meanes with any other, hath any power or authority to depose the King, or to dispose of his Majesty's kingdoms or dominions, or to authorize any forreigne prince to invade, or annoy him, or his country, or to discharge any of his subjects from their allegiance and obedience to his Majesty; or to give license or leave to any of them to beare armes, raise tumults, or offer any violence or hurt to his Majesty's Royall person, State or Government, or to any of his Majesty's subjects within his Majesty's dominions. Alsoe I doe sweare from my heart, that notwithstanding any declaration or sentence of ex-communication, or deprivation, made or granted, or to be made or granted by the Pope or his successors, or by any authority derived or pretended to be derived from him or his See against the said King, his heires or successors, or any absolution of the said subjects from their obedience, I will beare faith and true allegiance to his Majesty, his heires and successors, and him and them will defend to the uttermost of my power against all conspiracies and attempts whatsoever which shall be made against his or their persons, their Crowne and dignity, by reason or clause of any such sentence or declaration or otherwise, and will doe my best endeavour to disclose, and make knowne unto his Majesty, his heires and successors, all treasons and traiterous conspiracies, which I shall know or hear of, to be against him or any of them. And I doe further sweare that I doe from my heart, abhor, detest and abjure as impious and herritical, this damnable doctrine and position, that princes which be ex-communicated or deprived by the Pope, may be deposed or murthered by their subjects, or any other whatsoever. And I doe believe and in my conscience am resolved, that neither the Pope nor any person whatsoever, hath power to absolve me of this oath, or any part thereof, which I acknowledge by good and full authority to bee ministered unto me; and doe renounce all pardons and dispensations to the contrary. And all these things I doe plainly and sincerely acknowledge and sweare according to these express words by me spoken, according to the plaine and common sense and understandinge of the same words, without any equivocation or mentall evasion or secrett reservation whatsoever. And further, I doe here solemnly engage all true and loyall obedience unto his Majesty's authority placed and established in this his Collony of Rhode Island and Providence Plantations, and King's Province. And I doe make this recognition heartily, willingly, and truly, upon the true faith of a Christian. So help me God. [1679.]

No further oaths, or engagements, appear until the Administration of Sir Edmund Andros, in 1686, reduced the Colony to the nature of a County under his government.

In New Hampshire Colony.

As there was no constituted authorities over the patent of New Hampshire, the Exeter settlers, under the leadership of John Wheelwright, who had purchased a tract thirty miles square from certain Indian Sachems in April, 1638, were driven to the expedient of agreeing upon a voluntary association for governmental purposes. The executive and judicial functions were vested, in a board of three magistrates or elders, of whom the chief was styled Ruler. They were chosen by the whole body of freemen, who were the electors and legislators, their enactments, however, requiring the approval of the Ruler. An inhabitant had to be admitted a freeman, before he could enjoy the privileges of an elector. Under this association, an agreement was drawn up by the Reverend John Wheelwright, their leader, as follows:

THE COMBINATION FOR GOVERNMENT AT EXETER, WITH THE FORMS OF OATHS FOR RULERS AND PEOPLE

Whereas it hath pleased the lord to moue the heart of our Dread Soveraigne Charles by the grace of God, King of England, Scotland, France & Ireland, to grant license & liberty to sundry of his subjects to plant themselves in the Westerne partes of America: Wee, his loyall subjects, brethren of the church of Exeter, situate & lying upon the river of Piscataquacke, wh other inhabitants there, considering wth ourselves the holy will of god and our owne necessity, that we should not live w^thout wholsome lawes & government amongst us, of w^ch, we are altogether destitute; doe in the name of Christ & in the sight of god combine ourselves togethor, to erect & set up amongst us such government as shall be to our best discerning, agreeable to the will of god, professing ourselves subjects to our Soveraigne Lord King Charles, according to the libertys of our English Colony of the Massachusets & binding ourselves solemnely by the grace & helpe of Christ & in his name & feare to submit our selves to such godly & christian laws as are established in the realme of England to our best knowledge, & to all other such lawes wch shall upon good grounds be made & inacted amongst us according to god y^t we may live quietly & peaceably together in all godliness and honesty. Mon. 5th d., 4th, 1639. [John Whelewright, and thirty-four others.]

This was soon found to be unsatisfactory to some other settlers, who thought its expressions too lavish of loyalty to the King, and, in consequence, of prelacy; and while they were willing to acknowledge in a general way his sovereignty, and that they were his subjects, they had no disposition to make any unnecessary professions of allegiance. Another compact was then drawn of the same purport, simply acknowledging the King to be their Sovereign, and themselves his subjects. This was executed in due form and went into effect as the basis of government. But it did not bear the test of trial. Curiously, because it did not contain loyalty enough. And the original Combination was re-executed with the following explanatory preamble:

Whereas a certen combination was made by us, the brethren of the Church of Exeter, with the rest of the Inhabitants, bearing date Mon. 5th. d. 4, 1639, wh afterwards, upon the instant request of some of the brethren, was altered, & put into such a forme of wordes, wherein howsoever we doe acknowledge the King's Majesty our dread Sovereigne & ourselves his subjects: yet some expressions are contained therein wh may seeme to admit of such a sence as somewhat derogates from that due Allegiance wh we owe to his Highnesse, quite contrary to our true intents and meanings: We therefore doe revoke, disannull, make voyd and frustrate the said latter combination, as if it never had beene done, and doe ratify, confirme and establish the former, wh wee onely stand as being in force & virtue, the wh for substance is here set downe in manner and form following. Mon., 2d d., 2, 1640.

Both the Elders and the People were required to take certain prescribed oaths, as follows:

THE ELDERS OR RULERS OATH

You shall sweare by the great and dreadfull Name of the high God maker & Govr of heaven and earth, and by the Lord Jesus Christ ye Prince of the Kings and Rulers of the earth that in his name and feare you will Rule and Governe this people according to the righteous will of God's Ministering Justice and Judgm^t upon the workers of iniquity and Ministering due incurreagm^t and Countenance to well doers protecting of people so farre as in you by the helpe of God lyeth from forren Annoyance and inward disturbance that they may live a quiett and peacable life in all godlyness and honesty. So God bee helpful and gratious to you and yo^{rs} in Christ Jesus

The Oath of the People

Wee doe here sweare by the Great and dreadful name of y high God, maker and Gouern^r of Heaven & earth and by the Lord Jesus X ye King & Savio^r of his people that in his name & fear we will submitt o^r selves to be ruld & gouerned by, according to ye will & Word of God and such holsome Laws & ordinances as shall be derived theire from by O^r honr^d Rulers and ye Lawfull assistance with the consent of ye people and y wee will be ready to assist them by the helpe of God in the administration of Justice and p^{r}servacon of peace with o bodys and goods and best endeavo^{rs} according to God, so God protect & saue us and O^{rs} in Christ Jesus. [1640.]

The Combination of the People of Dover to Establish a Form of Government

Whereas sundry Mischiefes and inconveniences have befall us, and more and greater may in regard of want of Civil Government, his Gratious Matie haveing hitherto settled no Order for us to our knowledge:

Wee whose names are underwritten being inhabitants upon the River Piscataquack have voluntarilly agreed to combine our selves into a Body Politique that wee may the more comfortably enjoy the benefit of his Maties Lawes. And do hereby actually ingage our Selves to Submit to his Royal Matiei Lawes together with all such Orders as shalbee concluded by a Major part of the Freemen of our Society, in case they bee not repugnant to the Lawes of England and administered in the behalfe of his Majesty.

And this wee have mutually promised and concluded to do and so to continue till his Excellent Matie shall give other Order concerning us.

In Witness wee have hereto Set our hands the two & twentieth day of October in the sixteenth yeare of the Reign of our Sovereign Lord Charles by the grace of God King of Great Brittain France & Ireland Defender of the Faith &c. Anno Domi: 1640. [John Follett, and forty-one others.]

Under these forms the administration of the affairs of Exeter, and Dover, went on satisfactorily until, together with Hampton and Portsmouth, they came under the sway of Massachusetts-Bay in 1643; a part of the price the latter were ready to pay for the extension of their jurisdiction was that the citizens of the New Hampshire towns were to be allowed the elective franchise without reference to their being church members. This arrangement continued under the Laws of Massachusetts-Bay, as a part of Norfolk County, until New Hampshire became, in 1680, a Royal Province.

In the Generall Lawes and Liberties of the Province of New Hampshire, made by the Generall Assembly in Portsm° the 16th of March, 1679/80 and Aproved by the Presid[t] and Councill. The following is given as the status of

FREEMEN

8. It is ordered by this Assembly and the authority thereof y[t] all Englishmen being Protestants, y[t] are settled Inhabitants and freeholders in any towne of this Province, of y[e] age of 24 years, not viceous in life but of honest and good conversation, and such as have 201 Rateable estate w[th]out heads of persons having also taken the oath of allegiance to his Maj[s], and no others shall be admitted to y[e] liberty of being freemen of this Province, and to give theire votes for the choice of Deputies for the Generall Assembly, Constables, Selectmen, Jurors and other officers and concernes in y[e] townes where they dwell; provided this order give no liberty to any pson or psons to vote in the dispossion or distribution of any lands, timber or other properties in y[e] Towne, but such as have reall right thereto; and if any difference arise about s[d] right of voting, it shall be judged and determined by y[e] Presid[t] and Councill wth the Gen[ll] Assembly of this Province.

This Body of Laws when sent to England for Royal approval was disallowed.

In Province or County of Maine.

The Colonization of what is called in the Charter granted by Charles the First to Sir Ferdinando Gorges in 1639, "The Province or Countie of Mayne," presented many difficulties. The extraordinary governmental powers given to the Lord-Proprietary, which were transmissible with the property to his heirs and assigns, made of it a vast landed estate in which there could not be much voluntary co-operation. To assist in its government a board of Councilors was appointed who before taking office were required to "take the Oath of Allegiance according to the forme now used in this his highness' realme of England, and shall alsoe take the Oath hereunto subscribed."

Oath of Councilors of Province of Mayne

I do swear and protest before God Allmighty and by the holy contents of this Book to be a faithfull Servant and Councellor unto Sir Ferdinando Gorges Knight my Lord of the Province of Mayne, and to his heirs and assigns, to do and perform to the utmost of my power all dutiful respects to him or them belonging, concealing their Councells, and without respect of persons to do, perform and give my opinion in all causes according to my conscience, and best understanding both as I am a Councellor for hearing of causes, and otherwise freely to give him or them my opinion as I am a Councellor for matters of State or Common-wealths and that I will not conceal from him or them and their Councell any matter of conspiracy or mutinous practice against my said Lord and his heirs but will instantly after my knowledge thereof discover the same, and prosecute the authors thereof with all diligence and severity according to Justice, and thereupon do humbly kiss the Book. Taken September 2, 1639.

On the death of Sir Ferdinando in 1647, his estate in Maine passed to his son, John Gorges, who totally neglected his inheritance not even replying to repeated letters from the Gorges Colonists.

A Patent for lands on the Kennebeck River had been given to the New Plymouth Colony in 1629. In 1649, they let the trade upon it for a period of three years to Governor William Bradford, and four associates. In 1652, the trade was sold to the same men for three years longer. In that year, from actual survey, the east line of the Massachusetts-Bay Colony was found to encroach upon the liberties of the trade sold by and to the New Plymouth officers; and, in 1653, Thomas Prence was authorized to summon all and every inhabitant of the Kennebeck country to assemble and receive from him the instructions of the Plymouth General Court: "1. That the people should take the Oath of fidelity to the State of England, and to the government of New Plymouth. 2. That they were to be made acquainted with the Colony laws, applicable to them, and establish suitable rules and regulations to guide and govern them in their civil affairs. 3. None were to be inhabitants there but such as should take the Oath of Allegiance. 4. None could vote for an Assistant but such as should take the Oath."

The Oath required was in these words:

You shall be true and faithfull to the State of England, as it is now established, and whereas you chuse at present to reside within the government of New Plymouth, you shall not do, or cause to be done, any act, or acts, directly or indirectly by land or water, that shall, or may tend to the destruction or overthrow of the whole or part of this government, that shall be ordered, erected or established; but shall contrarywise, hinder, oppose, or discover such intents and purposes, as tend thereunto, to those that are in place for the time being; that the government may be informed thereof with all convenient speed; You shall also submitt, and observe all such good and wholesome laws, ordinances, and officers as are, or shall be established within the several limits thereof, So help you God, who is the God of Truth and the punisher of falsehood. [1653.]

This action constituted them freemen of Massachusetts, on taking the Oath, without the prerequisite of church membership. It was followed by a growing discontent against the chief officers in New Plymouth being lessees of the trade. The large returns which had been confidently expected were not being realized, and a jealousy of the people against those in power, finally led to the sale of the Patent, embracing seven hundred square miles, to a committee representing the Massachusetts-Bay Colony, for four hundred pounds.

In 1677, after much controversy and trouble with the heirs, Ferdinando Gorges, a grandson of the Lord-Proprietary, sold his rights to the Massachusetts-Bay Colony for one thousand two hundred and fifty pounds sterling, and the Territory of Maine became a District of Massachusetts down to the year 1820.

The power of an Oath is a subject for the Casuist. But, in the brief period of this paper—less than the span of life the Psalmist gives to man—we have seen an Oath throne and dethrone monarchs; build up and destroy flourishing Commonwealths; make and unmake Statehoods; be a guarantee of peace, and an incentive for war. Who, under these conflicting conditions, can measure their influence but Him in whose name and power they are made!

FAC-SIMILE OF ORIGINAL MANUSCRIPT
in the Handwriting of Thomas Dudley,
in the Public Library of the City of Boston

Issued with Bulletin, July, 1894

FAC-SIMILE OF ORIGINAL MANUSCRIPT
in the Handwriting of John Winthrop,
in the Public Library of the City of Boston
Issued with Bulletin, July, 1894

FACSIMILE OF ORIGINAL MANUSCRIPT RECORD

In the Handwriting of Secretary Simon Bradstreet
last Colonial Governor of Massachusetts Bay

Commissio- *ners for the* *united* *Colonies.*	WHERAS upon serious consideration, wee have concluded a confaederacie with the english Colonies of New-Plimouth, Conuecticot and New-Haven, as the bond of nature, reason, Religion and respect to our Nation doth require.
their power	Wee have this Court chosen our trustie and well-beloved friends (S.E.) and (W.H.) for this Colonie, for a full and compleat year, as any occasions and exigents may require and particularly for the next Meeting at (L.). And do invest them with full power and authoritie to treat, and conclude of all things according to the true tenour and meaning of the Articles of confoederation of the united Colonies, concluded at Bostone this ninth day of the third month 1643.
Oath of *fidelitie.*	I (A.B.) being by Gods providence an Inhabitant within the Jurisdiction of this Common wealth, doe freely and sincerly acknowledge my selfe to be subject to the Government therof. And doe heer sweare by the great and dreadfull Name of the Ever-living God, that I will be true and faithfull to the same, and will accordingly yeild assistance therunto, with my person and estate, as in equitie I ble bound; and will also truly indeavour to mainteine and preserve all the Liberties & Privuledges therof, submit- ting my self unto the wholsom Lawes made, & established by the same. And further, that I will not plot or practice any evil against it, or consent to any that shall soe doe, but will timely discover and reveal the same to lawfull Authoritie now heer established, for the speedy preventing therof. So help me God in our Lord Jesus Christ.
Freemans *Oath.*	I (A.C.) being by Gods providence an Inhabitant within this Jurisdiction of this Common-wealth, and now to be made free, doe heer freely acknowledge my self to be subject to the Government therof, and therfore doe heer sweare by the great and dreadfull Name of the Ever-living God, that I will be true and faithfull to the same, & will accordingly yeild assistance & support therunto, with my person & estate, as in equitie I am bound, and will also truly indeavour to mainteine & preserve all the Liber- ties and Privuledges therof, submitting my self unto the wholsom Lawes made and esta- blished by the same. And farther, that I will not plot or practice any evil against it, or consent to any that shall soe doe; but will timely discover & reveal the same to law- full authoritie now heer established, for the speedy prevention therof. Moreover, I doe solemnly binde my self in the sight of God, that when I shall be called to give my voice touching any such matter of this State, wherin Free-men are to deal, I will give my vote and suffrage as I shall in mine own conscience judge best to conduce and tend to the publick weal of the Body, without respect of persons, or fa- vour of any man. So help me God &c:
Governours *Oath.*	WHERAS you (A.B.) are chosen to the place of a Governour over this Jurisdi- ction for this year, and till a new be chosen & sworn; you doe heer swear by the Living God, that you will in all things concerning your place, according to your best power and skill, carie and deme in your self for the said time of your Governement, according to the Lawes of God, & for the advancement of his Gospel, the Lawes of this land, and the good of the people of this Jurisdiction. You shall doe justice to all men without partialitie, as much as in you lyeth: you shall not exceed the limitations of a Governour in your place. So help you God &c:
Deputie *Govr*	WHERAS you (A.B.) are chosen to the place of the Deputie-Governour &c: as in the Governours Oath, mutatis mutandis.

Wheras

FREEMAN'S OATH

Reproduced from "The Book of General Lawes and
Libertyes concerning the Inhabitants of the Massachusetts"—1648

By the courtesy of Henry Edwards Huntington

www.ingramcontent.com/pod-product-compliance
Lightning Source LLC
Chambersburg PA
CBHW052106270326
41931CB00012B/2905